HAVING IT ALL
OR NOT

Goals, Plans and Messages Work!

Linda M Gebhardt

HAVING IT ALL OR NOT
GOALS, PLANS AND MESSAGES WORK!

iUniverse books may be ordered through booksellers or by contacting:

iUniverse
1663 Liberty Drive
Bloomington, IN 47403
www.iuniverse.com
1-800-Authors (1-800-288-4677)

Because of the dynamic nature of the Internet, any web addresses or links contained in this book may have changed since publication and may no longer be valid. The views expressed in this work are solely those of the author and do not necessarily reflect the views of the publisher, and the publisher hereby disclaims any responsibility for them.

Any people depicted in stock imagery provided by Thinkstock are models, and such images are being used for illustrative purposes only. Certain stock imagery © Thinkstock.

ISBN: 978-1-5320-4149-5 (sc)
ISBN: 978-1-5320-4150-1 (e)

Library of Congress Control Number: 2018900564

Print information available on the last page.

iUniverse rev. date: 02/02/2018

Contents

Makes more sense to move forward than fight the forces pushing you backward. It's part of the human existence to resist growth. Fear—our worst enemy and greatest illustrator of all things possible—can be transformed into faith if we plant the seeds for forward momentum.

Acknowledgments:

Winslow Loomis
Helen Mason
Linda Strahle
Catherine Kelly
Lesley Reid Corydon
Douglas Brinker
Liz Kornicsky
Francis Ruth Whitlow

A quick-read story with several sagas, tales begging not to be forgotten—a riveting autobiography packed with essential scenes confessed in a narrative based on allowing you to identify with the theatre life exposes. Emotional excerpts of a mother, daughter, and wife and her experiences of success following the mantra; know what you want; nurture what you have and it will sow amazing results—let it go and *it* will most certainly fall into decay. Families and gardens are prime examples. Businesses and wealth are byproducts of stability. Not always. Your plans, goals and soul are the most empowering elements of living life.

Listening to first-class messages while discarding cheap insults is an x factor of life—more necessary than ever in history.

Hard to decipher which exact moment hinges on the next and relies on its predecessor as the defining moment of enlightenment—decisions assisting you to your perceived ascension to the throne. What makes us turn one way and not the other? What motivates us to make a decision at all?

Human's insatiable desire for freedom and certainty is an underlining theme and the reason why is more compelling. Most humans have a desire to have it all, or do we? How do we get there? *It* truly awards us a new perspective on the meaning of *things*. I hope this book inspires readers to reflect on all aspects of their lives and share tales, exalt in your own success and remind yourself why it's ok to succeed and fail.

Constant negativity in this world, breeds confusion. This book will make you wonder where your life is headed and extend the motivation that a plan is always an essential ingredient—at least it will keep your sanity. Positive messages are the fluid path to the soul and making sound decisions. Some of the visual funnies help illustrate, with emphasis, how laughter and focus have been a predominant coping mechanism throughout the years. Beats the bottle. We all have a story. The world is built on stories—not algorithms.

Beside signing up for the one-way trip to Mars, there must be a sexier option than becoming a Martian. To live in fear is not living. To adapt to the new world order with a perspective on the journey may soothe the nerves. At least we may learn the meaning of our *things*. These pages were written, rewritten and edited with the help of the funniest people I know on the planet. Promise.

The soul is the most indelible possession we own, yet our world dictates that we keep it guarded.

The promise of the message: You can do it. You need a plan if you even remotely possess any goals and a system for gleaning the positive messages from those that desire to see you shine and discard the destructive insults. The book may enlighten you to the difference–the result may find you currently having it all—*it* may be right in front of you. Time to nurture your good fortune, abandon the damaging messages including the worn-out baggage and begin to live according to your plan and solid system for unleashing the stress you loathe and the freedom each of us crave. Even a small plan is the most empowering gift you can give yourself wrapped in a renewed enthusiasm for all of life's offerings as you continually motivate to move your life forward.

Reviews

Excellent read. Life constantly throws curveballs and this book reveals a woman's struggles and success to stay relevant in a ever changing world. Not only is the writing superbly crafted but the messages along the way are powerful and insightful. It has motivated me to remember who I was before I became engrossed in my children's lives. Time to get back in the game and reinvent myself. Cant wait to get the business plan as its all about having the proper plan!! Thank you to the author for the motivation and insight! Just what I needed!!

Catherine Kelly, *entrepreneur, Chicago*

"A fun read with a message, not to be missed!"

A. Loomis

Especially dedicated to my brother
Michael, Amelia and Dimitri

*Because beyond all else we must retain
hope. Hope and faith extinguish fear.*

*Angels will always appear, look for them, they
typically are not white with wings and halos.*

"Things are as they are supposed to be," she says. "I am still here, never too old so long as I breathe to wonder, to learn, and to teach."

— Caroline Stoessinger. Holocaust survivor

"We learn by doing. Only knowledge that is used sticks in your mind."

— Dale Carnegie

1

....

Freedom

The scene was not particularly impressive by any standard, however as my parents watched and listened at the window, five girls, all high school graduates sat in a Vega crying at the curb of my house as we bid farewell to each other in the late summer of 1978. Each of us venturing to different colleges, opposite directions and a colorful journey. The scene was iconic. From a parent's perspective in the second story window, the visual must have been frightening due to the uncertainty and fear it had to release. Exulting for my brothers who were most likely fighting in the background over who took the extra bedroom now that SHE will be gone. To me, it meant not moving around a small house under my parent's glare. Freedom at last. If I truthfully recorded all the details of growing up with 4 brothers the best souvenir and recap are the scars on my knees and face. Who does plastic surgery on their knees? The scar on my face occurred while we were young and playful. It would never be removed for fear the memory might vanish. Being hit with a steel shovel all in the name of fun in the winter in Chicago in the 60's—why would you eradicate that symbol? From my mother's point of view, raising 5 kids tightly packed in age, she didn't reach for her coat to head to the hospital until she heard the 5th Band-Aid being opened. We all knew the 6th Band-Aid meant stitches.

All that behind me, we piled into the blazing hot family station wagon and drove to Kansas in August. Each cornfield of the 500-mile drive to St. Mary College was like watching stripes on a tiger and hoping it doesn't leap out and bite. Another cornfield—how far away was this school? The freedom I looked forward to was now gripping my stomach without letting go and the brash reality of being alone reared its ugly head. I was scared.

How did I even choose a small, all-girl Catholic college in Leavenworth, Kansas much less even locate one? It was Helen's fault. Senior year in high school I received an invitation to explore the possibilities at a small intimate school. Hummm. Curiosity and exploring tendencies were never my short-fall. I obliged the invitation. Upon arrival, Helen, already a freshman, greeted our group instantly attaching to a kindred spirited friend who could mobilize a crowd and create a consensus immediately. She won me over with her worldly prowess, beautiful lightly manicured, curly brown hair and deep voice accompanied with assured posture. In other words, I was impressed and sold within the first hour. St. Mary College, became the front-runner for schools including a nice scholarship to enhance the deal.

The first week of college-life, I met some of the most intriguing people on the planet and that says alot coming from a city of 6 million plus. The antics were not a pretty scene but oh so fun. The first semester tales are from the curious side of life yet resemble the dark side. Schoolwork was just a prop reminding me that I was in school after all. Coming of age in college was not the goal—being free was more worthy of my attention. Yet this school became a challenge aggravating me to adhere to the rules which I knew my high school friends in college were not experiencing. Boys were strictly forbidden on the floors except to check-in at the front desk—similar to a hospital. Or on some days felt more like a funny farm. The school was all-girls, very Catholic and included friends today that are truly special. Only three of them—Helen, Winslow and Maureen. Thirty-five years later we still recall the mischief we caused and why the other girls at the school referred to us as the popular girls. Everyone else in this scenic school in Leavenworth, Kansas, with a well-lit view of the federal penitentiary out the dorm room window, we categorized as weirdos. It was hard to take things too seriously here while envisioning going out into the real world and making something of yourself beside being a feminist who enjoyed leaning in on men.

The natural environment and serene hilly landscape with

original brick mile-long drive to the main entrance made it appear as though it was planted there by some Gatsby-like benefactor. Stately until you entered and the smell of its age eluded a familiar scent—like grandma's apartment in the city when you ascended the stairs to the third floor. Musty from the carpet treads and a 100 years of humidity locked into its history. Best part—it was familiar, thus I was able to attach to something other than not remembering why this whole thing of college was a right of passage and any other option was not presented. I was locked in—literally.

"Keep going Linda, you decided this school was a good idea. You might as well join in and entertain yourself. What else do you have?" I mumbled these words and ruminated thoughts of escaping my disastrous selection of colleges. Schoolwork never presented a severe challenge coming from a high school of 4000 and going to a remote school of under 1000.

Helen and I had been bonded from the past year's initiation, and today the privilege was meeting her sister, Maureen, also a freshman and her friend

Winslow. These two raving beauties would form the popular girls as we became referred to in the hallowed halls of school, even though the term meant the hair on my neck would bristle. Another reminder an all-girls school and its iconic gesture was such a bad idea.

However, on this meet and greet day a certain joy came through and my first impression of Maureen and Winslow was positive to the point of, "I can handle this school if they are as fun as they look." Winslow, although it was discovered later didn't really care for me at first introductions, had amazing blonde, thick hair and the color of her eyes were like a clear cloudless sky. Eyelashes that seemed to extend forever and a dreamy southern accent like from a movie, however I couldn't recall which one. Included in this first impression was an ethereal beauty to her demeanor, yet my big city-suspicion took over and loudly resonated: there's more to the story —I liked her.

Maureen spoke without speaking: a beautiful red-head with perfect skin who knew how to manufacture fun. Like her sister, a bold quality that said let's not waste any time the boys are out there we have to go to them.

The popular girls knew we were doomed to fail in this environment. But, we proceeded to get good grades, try and follow the rules and make sure we left on the weekends. It was Helen's fault, again. Prior to our arrival our freshman year, Helen was a sophomore and knew these fabulous boys from the east coast, football players at Washburn University in Topeka, Kansas who knew the meaning of collegiate fun. I was game.

Being dis-illusioned my first semester, and what made it bearable, was the trouble all four of us caused. And lots of it—seemed like it followed us around. Not necessarily committing felonies that landed you in jail—it felt like jail because you were grounded for doing ridiculous things. Like checking out the school car and not bringing it back on time.

"Oh, aren't we are supposed to bring it back before sundown? It is sundown. What's the problem?"

"Yes, Linda, it's two days late." Oopsy.

It didn't go unnoticed that the popular girls brought the big 'ole Chevy to Topeka on Friday and returned it on Sunday by sundown. Yes, I was grounded in college—it's amazing they didn't make me wear white gloves and patent-leather shoes to class similar to our predecessors who graduated from St. Mary's in the 50's. The punishment meant not being able to leave the campus for 4 weeks. Somehow I weaseled it down to two weeks—a strategy that was growing old—how to get out of your punishments. Keep in mind it's 1978.

Grounded for doing things like entertaining boys up on our floor on mixer dance night. The first mixer of the semester was a dance in the gym with the boys from Benedictine

College—all boys of course and a bus load of them. The visceral notion of interested in Benedictine boys anyway, our attention became fixed on the boys from Topeka and all the foolishness they served.

2

Something Is Not Right

Parents are always excited to pick up their children after the first semester in college. My swell sight included two black eyes—pretty is as pretty does. The result of a horrific accident I should have died in, yet an angel appeared and the transcendence of the memory is having no recollection of the horrid details. There were 6 of us, 2 boys and 4 girls, in a Gremlin trying to outrun an oncoming train—and yes, we were drinking. Avoiding the collision, we smacked a telephone pole straight on. My synopsis of this event is more stimulating than the result—going to St. Mary college was great for my grades, not for my advancement in this world. Having boys come to the school and take us off campus developed into a life-threatening event.

By second semester, a feeling of stuck became overwhelming. An anxiety attack was new to me and the worst part of having one is not knowing what or where it originates. As a second semester freshman seeking counseling, it really didn't change anything or that awful crumpled-up-in-a-ball feeling. Perhaps the disconnect with normal collegiate school life compared to my friends from Chicago was a contributing factor. Again, the answers were elusive and the solution seemed like it would never happen. Confusion ensued, yet I made it through another semester with B or above grades and the revelation that school was the logical route to pursue. However, this school, supposedly steeped in tradition was not how I pictured collegiate life. What I witnessed looked like scenes from *One Flew Over the Cuckoos Nest*. Students cutting themselves, first roommate telling me she was possessed (in retrospect she probably was), loners and my select fun friends that kept me there for lack of an option. My parents, being the forever-Catholics weren't going to see my point of view on changing schools. In other words, college students are supposed to be perfect in making all the right decisions, and not play victim to the vicissitudes of living.

Sentimental and psychological ties between my girlfriends at St. Mary and the boys in Topeka were tugging at my soul by this time. The school was just a backdrop. Ruminating as to why Billy and Helen's relationship became strong and a force unknown, caused much angst. William Arthur, or Billy as we called him, an attraction to all of us, became a symbol of the real world and college at this point in time. A linebacker at Washburn University in Topeka, he looked every bit the part. The image of him and his no-nonsense, no smile, I'll kick your ass if I don't like your style typified his whole existence. He would have made a dangerous poker player. To me he was Helen's boyfriend and despite his distrust of many people he really enjoyed me—I referred to him as my bodyguard. Broad shoulders, dark hair, deep Boston accent and a frozen stare that said, "I only speak when I decide." He was the commander-in-chief and if he was ginned up watch out. Looking for trouble, we were the spectators with a feeling like watching a ten car pile-up—you couldn't take your eyes off the scene. It became a sorry excuse for entertainment that usually ended up with a fight he always won.

More schoolwork and more antics piled up at SMC. The next mixer our friends from Topeka decided to come up to Leavenworth and check out the scene and the girls (weirdos) all for themselves. I didn't have a good feeling things were going to end well—and they didn't. Helen and I had the go-to room with its cool murals, a powder room minus the toilet not to mention the corner room, the largest room on the fourth floor. Someone had the bright idea we could sneak Billy up to the room so he could finally check out his girlfriend's enclave. This didn't go unnoticed by the higher-ups who knew we were up to something. Thus, while Billy received the 10 second tour, I alerted them to the sound of Otis, the 100-year old elevator opening on our floor.

"Billy hide in the sink room." thinking to myself 'they wouldn't look there?' The nuns weren't stupid—that was the

9

first place they looked. I laid on my bed and tried to harness my laughter. We're dead.

"Hi, I'm the plumahr," Billy greeted them with certainty and his thick New England accent. Penance time for Helen and I.

Time for the third semester in college and each of us including Winslow, Helen and Maureen managed to save enough money over the summer to pool our meager earnings together, buy a car and split it four ways ignoring any messy details that might crop up. Winslow and I happened to arrive in Kansas first, dedicating ourselves the special privilege of purchasing the getaway car. Needless to say we knew nothing about used cars and everything about what a car represented to our soul. Basically, we were highly motivated buyers, blonde and the used car salesman must have seen us running to the lot while we counted the money from three blocks away.

A red Vega with 4-speed transmission. We neglected to ask the other two owners, in their absence, if they knew how to drive a manual car. Oh well; cheap car, ran, transported us to the liquor store and off to Topeka to see our boys. The rules: everyone going to Topeka had to equally share the gas money. Typically, it would cost $4.00 to get us from Leavenworth to Topeka. $5.00 was a more comfortable amount to ensure we weren't going to run out of gas at the Topeka exit off Interstate 70 in case we had some unimaginable detour. Oh, what could possibly go wrong?

The car could hold five which meant occasionally we'd recruit girls from the school as eye wash for the boys—it was the least we could do as we were their guests at their house. They tried to like our selection, but weren't impressed. Our friends from the east coast became a tough crowd to please and girls we recruited didn't get the attraction. What snobs. After all, how could you not get excited to enter a house with holes in the walls, stolen steaks and my personal favorite:

extra cheese on the eggs? Found furniture, not from Ethan Allen and one working bathroom which invoked many a fight as someone always used too much hot water. Winslow and I went to McDonald's to the bathroom. A specially crafted plan came in handy when we bought the car—we were the only two that knew how to drive a stick.

One weekend during our typical routine of 5 girls stopping at the liquor store conning our buddy to allow us to buy liquor, we jumped back into the car and elected Winslow to go into the gas station and purchase the necessary gas to get us to Topeka. Five dollars was collected, or so we thought. Someone else pumped the gas and proceeded to put $5.00 in the tank. Packed tightly in the car and ready for the ride we drove not more than a half a mile and the lights of a cop car were behind us. I was driving and certain that speeding wasn't the issue here.

"Oh please God, don't let it be the Mad Dog," murmuring to myself.

"What seems to be the problem officer?"

I turned down the window just enough to speak as my drum-beat-pounding heart knew something was very wrong.

"You put $1.00 more of gas in the car than you paid for." And we all proceeded to fight amongst ourselves and point fingers while the cop scratched his head at the hen fight ensuing inside the tiny packed car.

"We think it was Winslow," Helen said assured that this would get us out of any jail time. Her pristine look of innocence, white-blonde hair perfectly curled and batting her mile-long eyelashes determined we could point the finger directly at Winslow.

"Please, just turn around and go back to the station and pay the man the additional dollar." We were lucky this time— we had the extra dollar.

Where our luck began to turn was when the nuns and the president of the school took notice of our every move.

Helen and I were artists and by this time, roommates. Being popular was an illusion because the administration did not care for our antics or our artwork. The very cool murals on the walls of our room were done in oil pastel chalk. Mine was colorful and the layers of thick oil pastels made it a tourist attraction among the other students not to mention a point of contention for the faculty. The popular girls were losing steam and fast.

"Why are the murals a problem?" I asked Sister Mary Janet who was the president and headed up the committee to renovate this historical school. I called the meeting because Helen and I were being charged for our lovely artwork to be removed. Harsh.

"Won't our murals be a reminder of all the creative girls who have walked these halls and thought for themselves?" Undeniably, I was grabbing at straws and coming up short. It was a scene similar to any relationship that has hit an impasse and you both know parting ways is for the best. However, digging in and having the last word seems to make the transition bearable or at the very least there isn't an uncontested winner or loser just for the record.

We argued our point of view for several minutes without a conclusion.

"Linda, don't you think you and your popular girls would be happier somewhere else?" Sister Janet asked with one eye on me and the other on her notes. Uh oh. Was I being kicked out or graciously led to the door?

"Yes, but how will I tell my parents?" I sulked.

Game over. It was time to search for a new school and the daunting task of what to say and why. Not to mention where were we going?

3

··

A Real School

The University of Kansas became our unanimous vote. Oh yes, all four of us and the special little Vega trooped down Interstate 70 and applied at KU. This option had some long-term appeal to me, yet we were all accepted based solely on the fact that we weren't dumb girls. By now, the Vega was omitting fumes and the clutch, after much torment from those who learned how to drive a manual transmission, approaching its last leg.

Collectively, this move was in Helen and my favor, because KU had a well renowned art and design department. The university represented the next step in school combined with my leash appeared to be growing longer. I actually researched whether they grounded students at KU. No, but the harrowing realities of going to a large school and buckling down combined with graduating "on time" became the focus. This was the real world now—time to pay closer attention to the details and shelve freedom in return for reasonable grades and redemption in my parent's eyes. We made the switch in the spring semester of 1980. Or, just in the nick of time before we were all officially kicked out of St. Mary's College.

"Isn't this the best art and design school —all the provisions of real life, Helen?" squealing in delight on the second day of classes. Most notably we were all surviving like the arrival of outcasts in a far-away land. I didn't feel adrift and alone, but the disconnect with Helen and our new school was percolating. Something was amiss. Helen appeared to be floundering and I was flourishing—not the predictable outcome. However, I vowed to transform myself and make my way in this new environment.

"Helen, you're not even trying," reaching out to understand why she wasn't feeling the same relief existing in this seemingly appropriate environment away from the cruel world of St. Mary's. The semester was only two weeks old.

"I'm pregnant," you could see it in her eyes, "and I'm

ill and Billy is the father." Again, life came to a standstill for exactly 10 minutes. She became the person I scarcely recognized laying on the couch in a blue robe sleeping off the school day. This was unfamiliar territory and not how we predicted our epic tale to end. The popular girls seemed like a million years ago.

"What are you going to do?" I was scared as the devil seemed to be lurking again in my life. Billy was handsome and my first naive statement for lack of anything else to say, "That baby will be beautiful"! Duh.

The new journey at KU began to feel like a variation on the path we left behind. However, perseverance and tenacity allowed me to show myself what I had and being the supportive person my reply to Helen, "you have what it takes to be a great mother knowing an abortion is not even remotely an option."

Wanting to verbalize but silently thinking, "It sucks to be you unless a baby at 20 and all the responsibilities of a life change was how you pictured things."

Winslow, Maureen and I kept our rental house in Lawrence, finished the semester, ditched the car in a parking lot and to this day, some thirty-five years later, have no idea the poor soul that Vega ended up with. Hopefully it treated the new owner with as much fun and diversion and continued to facilitate more stories including setting someone free. Always wished I had left a note with the abandoned car. After all, cars have emotional value too and this one was packed to the brim. Nothing incriminating, just a simple yet perplexing note for the newbie of the Vega:

Thanks for being there for us while we bowed to your existence.

This car is free for its new owner—Free being the operative word. It set 4 girls on a journey that otherwise could have been a slippery slope. Enjoy.

Helen and Billy quit school and moved to Boston living with his parents in Lynn, Massachusetts. A rough area adjacent to the city and an equally hellacious time for both of them considering they were starting a family without a degree or meaningful jobs, not to mention a roof over their head wasn't certain. Remembering several discussions, while we were roommates, of the real world, pontificating for hours the true definition of the real world from our point-of-view. Easy to do from a dorm room's snuggly bed, three squares right downstairs and parents that were paying for it. All the ideas and philosophy were just an illusion. Yet, I somehow envisioned Helen making it.

Freedom now had a steep price tag. Schoolwork was challenging and I lost my reason for being in Kansas in the first place. Forgetting is adaptive after all and I became complacent in dismissing all that happened at St. Mary's as though it never did. Thus the strategy was to seek new heroes and mentors.

Simultaneously, my bond with Winslow grew quite strong taking more notice of her soothing voice and beautifully balanced features. Winslow was from Athens, Georgia and her mother had gone to St. Mary College back in the 1950s. Likewise, she was currently contemplating why Kansas was the right choice when the University of Georgia was within walking distance of the house she grew up in. We bonded famously discovering each of us had a wickedly funny trait and together our point of view became hilarious—at least to us. This specialty was essential because our chapter and verse in college was now going to take a new spin. How were we going to make all new friends? Winslow was drop dead beautiful. I, wouldn't describe myself that way—just cute.

It didn't take long—oh maybe about one more week after the ditching-the-car incident. Winslow and I knew our outdated formula for finding friends didn't go so well in the last school. Maureen was on her own path to crafting an exit out of KU completely. Helen and Billy were in Boston and I was growing attached to my fellow design students, a new boyfriend, and a new path to prosperity—all this combined to soothe the nervousness of the newness.

The to-do list arrived through the left side of my brain. The discovery of my innate need to control my destiny, fashionably referred to as growing up, forced the right side of my brain to shut down. The list looked like this:

1. Focus.
2. Graduate on time.
3. Make the work this entails enjoyable.
4. Please parents.

"Lynn, are you going to be able to handle all this new maturity?" Winslow's sarcasm was never boring and typically worth noting.

"Oh, probably not, but I have to, the alternative visual is ugly."

"Yes, it is Lindseydo," my nickname from St. Mary's.

"And, Eunice what are your goals?" My favorite choice of nicknames for Winslow when we had these bouts of nervous laughter that seemed to originate from parts unknown.

"I don't have any," and she smiled that look emblazoned in my head which signified the rewards of change were completely uncertain. Our bond spoke to me and said it was more sarcastic than truthful.

"Good idea," with pure joy in my heart that she was not going to ditch out on me and run back to Athens. We were immersed in this new journey at Kansas University together—for now. We had a lot of ground to make up since we were no sharper or inspired than the day we arrived at St. Mary's.

Again, school was good to me this first semester at this gargantuan school, as I truly possessed the power of bullet point number 1. Focus. Just like my list read and I followed along like a true soldier never deviating from the 4 simple bullet points. That was the goal at least, always pining for very little oscillation on the journey to graduation.

After a summer of diligently working in Chicago there cropped up an uncertainty of whether Winslow would be returning for junior year at KU. She returned with an iron and some knickknacks or whatever she could fit into a large suitcase.

"Win, we have to find an apartment and furnish it ourselves. We can't cook dinner with this dried flower arrangement and soap dish. What else did you have coming?"

"Nothing."

"Oh." The good news for us—everyone loved Winslow. My collection of design friends, Kevin, Perry, Julie, and Rob, bold and imaginative people, couldn't help but love her and come to our rescue. Perry, the forever-artist donated a set of flaming orange round plastic chairs we used in the living room of the one-bedroom apartment on campus. We bought two used, full-size mattresses and laid them on opposite ends of the humble bedroom. The couch was some flea-bitten castaway from Kevin's fraternity we fumigated with baby powder. Not exactly a solid infrastructure for learning, but we managed.

A life-changing cast of spirited friends assembled in the School of Fine Arts forming a reliable foundation. Each was truly able to ignite my passion for graphic design and the promise it might deliver after graduation.

Problem is, I should have made the list, which was now 6 months old, into a tattoo similar to a backup system like sailors have handy if their compass isn't reliable. A black tattoo in 24 point Helvetica Extra Bold on my forearm would've been way more effective. Otherwise, the temptation to jumble up the order of the list and misfire was precariously high. With school under control, graduating on time was looking achievable, it follows that bullet point number 3 and the word enjoyable became THE focus.

Wanderlust climbed back into my bones. I morphed into a seasoned pro rationalizing why traveling is important to living. Back in the day, visual communication majors better known today as graphic designers and illustrators, "should be curious and experience the world around you," our renowned teachers preached. This rhetoric was all I needed to convince myself and anyone within earshot why we had to explore—now! Fixated on this revelation, daydreaming of faraway places juxtaposed a part of my school day. After all, I possessed a bare honesty in my voice when speaking of travel and not the grandiloquence of a lunatic who is eager to get off the reservation. Some of my friends payed attention—most didn't. I came to the conclusion it was about time to treat my human spirit to a reward for the unwavering dedication to schoolwork and all the positive choices. Not necessarily that the cynosure of images conjured up needed to be replaced with adventure, I developed an insatiable desire to "see".

Being able to see is noteworthy because the how-to evolves into a skill. If the steps of formulating meaning of what you see entails one thousand steps —I was at step one.

Two weeks had passed since this fixation occurred. This fine Saturday night in February, med students were having a party in Kansas City hosted by Perry's best friend Steve, also a gifted med student. An environment only true designers could love. Braniacs with eccentric points of view—smart, funny and precocious combined with bow ties, crisp shirts and ironed jeans. We didn't have time to iron our jeans in art school for that matter we didn't own an iron. It was beyond my comprehension on how students of the sciences could even find the precious time to drink. It was worth exploring. After a few cocktails Mel, a med student said, "my parents would love to have you guys stay with them in Rockville Center on Long Island." Like the speed of an east African gazelle I joined the conversation and engaged in what it took to make the trip happen. The fine art of eavesdropping, I developed, was about to yield riches. We, always assuming I'm on the invite list, began immediate preparations which included the appropriate car to drive and how we would manage to leave the next day and not waste another minute. Steve, Perry and I obliged and decided the most operable car to put to this task was Steve's Mazda Rx7. Perry and I drove back to KU that night in order to pack on Sunday morning. We proceeded to go to the laundromat and wash all the clothes necessary for the trip.

While we were washing the clothes in downtown Lawrence, Winslow was walking back to our apartment from work and noticed us in the laundromat with open suitcases.

"What are you doing, Lindseydo?"

"We're washing clothes so we can leave straight from here and go to New York City. I know this doesn't make sense, but I'm too excited to say no." She had no idea this plan was in motion, unfortunately she missed the party.

"You're crazy!" she shrieked. "Do your parents know? What did your teacher's say? What are you going to do about missing all that school? I can't watch." With her even-keeled demeanor surfacing and a smirk on her face she said, "something about this sounds fun—wish I had the guts to do it, too!"

"Cool, that's what I'll tell my parents. You thought it was a good idea."

My family loved Winslow. I was armed with all the rationale needed to pull off this excursion with minimal outside pressure. She twisted my ear, pursed her lips and walked out. A familiar reaction.

"I'll bring you a souvenir, Eunice! Love you!"

Immediately after the suitcase was stuffed with clean clothes, we proceeded to Kansas City to pick up Steve in his car. From Kansas City to New York City a snow storm aggravated us most of the 2000 miles. Reluctant to admit this whole idea was a farce, we arrived in Rockville Center and the intensity of the here-we-are feeling dismissed any doubt.

Procuring smart travel buddies becomes the essential of any adventure. Just in case disaster strikes in New York City, Perry and Steve were sharp and the security this provided made the trip flawless. A lesson learned. This safeness provided the armor needed to talk our way around certain obstacles.

For example, we had little money between us and large eyes for the finer things in NYC. Broadway was of particular interest, except tickets for a show were well beyond our means. That didn't stop me. I had a plan and the boys concurred it was worth a try.

At the ticket booth on 42nd street, in the drizzle of a fine rain, I walked up to the attendant and pleaded our case. We had our hearts set on A Chorus Line and my acting prowess was about to emerge.

"We're design students [white lie—Steve was a med student enjoying a full scholarship and the promise of a medical degree by 24 years old], and we took it upon ourselves to leave Kansas to explore the city," I said with a sheepish grin and a heart-felt believability the attendant enjoyed. "How about we just stand in the back and watch. We'll be quiet as a mouse and no one will notice. Pllleeease. If we talk, you can boot us out immediately no questions." The passion in my voice attached to a soul that was on fire did the trick.

"How much money do you have?" he asked.

"25.00 total. Sorry. You won't regret this." Acting like I was somebody.

"Ok. I can't believe I'm doing this, but you can have 3 standing-room only tickets for the 2:00 p.m. matinee. You'll make a fine businesswoman someday ma'am." All of 20 years old, there was no meaning in the magnitude of this statement—yet.

I stood there and small tears were welling up with an adrenaline pumping feeling never before experienced. A magical sensation.

Saying goodbye to NYC, we decided that our return trip should include a pit stop in Chicago.

"Staying with my parents may soothe their nerves," I said assuredly.

It was easy to talk my buddies into delaying school for one more day. Of course, my parents were thrilled to meet the new partners in crime. The most rewarding part of the Chicago portion of the one-day stay: I admired my mom and dad for understanding my artsy point-of-view and that all my ideas were not half-baked—there was a purpose and a reason but it hadn't surfaced yet. One less pressure to deal with as the arduous task of talking to my design teachers and other faculty was a grim reminder of similar antics at St. Mary's, however the consequences were not clear. "I'll think of something!"

"10 days off to see the design capital of the world would be beneficial to graduating well-rounded." That's how I'd start off the explanation. Not to mention they didn't learn of this excursion until after we got back from the east coast. I had a lot of convincing ahead of me and mounds of unfinished projects and due dates. Ugh.

One of my favorite friends and boyfriend, Kevin, was more enamored with my nonsensical behavior than my looks. We enjoyed each other in the tasks and discipline it took to enter and finish at the School of Fine Arts. The plan was to be the best. And then try and be better than the best. KU had some of the greatest professors of design in the United States as I discovered after accidentally enrolling. Luck was on my side, as the distinctly peculiar people in the VAB (Visual

Arts Building) were just normal enough to fuel the drive to succeed. A fine assortment that ignited my competitive spirit. After a trip to see other worlds I became passionate, focused and worked 24/7 on my visual communication career figuring it was a small down payment on my future. These were not easy nights and days. School at a highly competitive art school became a bear and having a boyfriend to lean on was a precious commodity. Kevin was competitive with a burning desire to set the art world on fire. He always encouraged me to do the same, although in retrospect burning is not the essential word for success. Clearly, differentiation is what mattered, or so I hypothesized. Seeking the accoutrements of a well-rounded, marketable designer, the search was on for something more—a discerning point that makes me stand out without appearing unzipped.

Springing into action, the summer before senior year in college, I reached for the yellow pages and started dialing. I had the one-up on my design friends returning to Chicago for summer work.

Beginning with the A's, the plan was to phone all the ad agencies in Chicago and ask if there was any need for a junior designer. The fourth agency was The Ad Agency. Score.

"We really only need a key liner. But, you never know there may be an occasion where we need some design work," the art director on the other line said with a reassurance that a job was possible.

"Can I come in tomorrow and talk?" knowing that key liners were the bottom rung on the ladder of success for a design career. Drek work, however my motivation rotated to a competitive nature and the focus was on how to get ahead early in the game. Working with the disadvantage of changing schools and not all of the credits compiled for a march across the stage in May of 1982 for commencement pomp and circumstances, I was in a year-long mad scramble for appropriate credits.

My parent's had envisioned graduation day since I was born and were properly preparing for this day for four years. After all, it was promised. Certain that my mom was already shopping for a suitable outfit, and Dad was boasting of the first child in the family receiving a degree—I better shift into high gear. Bullet point number four—please parents was not forgotten.

After an arduous summer of key-lining without any regrets to the dedication served to my employers, I knew this last year in school needed to link the past three years of focused schoolwork, travel, unique personal intensity and decent grades to get the piece of paper—better known as a degree. The actual paper had no special meaning other than something to doodle on. I envisioned a paycheck sprinkled with adventure.

The first semester of senior year was dreamy. I had been selected into THE ARTS program bestowed on the select gifted designers at KU. Wow. My own office in the school and a break from our musing in the workroom about life after school. Beside, it meant a scholarship for tuition. I was cool because this became the point of entry into the world of external validation from the public eye. Time to take a bow and revel in greatness. And right after I jumped down off my high horse it was essential to get to work. Hard work. Lesson learned: You are only as good as your performance the next day. It's like hitting a home run at a picnic softball game and forgetting to run the bases because you are so enamored by your greatness you got stuck in the moment and carried the bat to home plate—barely. Every day had to be a home run in THE ARTS program.

In today's world of "computers do everything" we did not have this luxury. Not even close. Everything in print was done by hand. Dating myself, for those who can relate to "back in the day", you needed to know how to draw a straight line by hand. 35+ years ago all print design and advertising was produced with a T-square, plastic or steel triangle, Luci, stat cameras, hand-drawing curves, rapidiographs, exacto knives, the noxious smell of rubber cement, benzene (gasoline) to clean your hands and a fastidious mind to make the output happen. In other words, the hand and mind were tightly related and mistakes happened often. Discipline, perfection and patience were essential ingredients to the creative process. An idea was 10% of what you saw in the newspaper or magazines. The whole process was similar to digging a ditch and making the walls perfect. We were warned that a future boss may watch over the process and decide if circuitous routes were used for the sole purpose of avoiding a step. Otherwise, known as being a lazy designer. False. Best to learn early on the fine art of discipline. Being average was not acceptable in the competitive world of differentiation.

Point well taken, the most valuable tool in the kit was going to be absolutely stunning samples of the process. THE ARTS allowed us to work with real clients, produce printed work for the theatre at the university and have a portfolio saying, "that's what I did." Necessary for the real world was how all this beautiful artwork elevated the bottom line for a corporation. Ah, that should be easy how could anyone not like pretty things—hedging my offerings would be in demand. In my naive world a recession was a disappearing hairline.

One more semester to go and the need to grow richer through travel nudged at me once again. My best friend from high school, Karen phoned and invited me to her dad's condo on the beach in the Virgin Islands over Christmas break of 1981-82, flattered at the invitation.

"You just need to pay for the plane ticket, Lynn."

"How will I pull this off?" dreaming of faraway places with one of my bold and daring friends who knew the precise definition of having a good time. Worried that it deviated too far from the four bullet points, most notably please parents, and nearing graduation with a few credits short, I said "Yes".

Seeking a perfect predictable life was old-fashioned. A finite skill for unconventionally solving problems began to arise. First order of business was how to tell my parents. Solved. They were very good friends with Karen's dad, Jim and his second wife Susie and concurred it was an opportunity of a lifetime. Of course, not mentioning that it threatened graduation on time, I'd cross that bridge when it came up. This trip was going to be practice for the real world.

Another skillful qualification for entering the job market: believable rationalization in exchange for adventure. Where would that line item go on the resume? I conveniently paid close attention when teachers taught us to be continuously curious.

This trip, beyond going to the Caribbean in the dead of winter, would include the delivery of kinetic excitement of laughter, men and fine food. It also promised that edge of culture necessary to enhance my limited perceptions of the world. We were on our way to another country.

Upon opening the door of the small by-plane, the whiff of fresh tropical air engaged your senses and became the instant chill pill. Traveling by car up to the cliff where the condo sat, this island appeared to be a birder's paradise with every imaginable color of singing birds on trees with matching fluorescent flowers. As twilight was beginning the surreal hues of pink, violet and orange silhouetted the out-islands like varying sizes of bee hives. Warm air that induced a relaxation response —beats school. Karen and I lounged the first night and began reading a shark book of all things. As we planned our itinerary into uncharted adventure, we were ready for all possibilities. We were known to challenge each other with dares in our high school dalliances. One species I did not flirt with was a shark or any large fish—it was off limits. The good news; the crystal clear water allowed for any fish to expose themselves from a great distance. Yeah, like I could swim faster than a fish, but clarity became the reality if swimming was on the agenda and sure enough a sailboat cruise with snorkeling off-shore was the crowd favorite for day 1 activities. Eager to act like an islander, I shut down my nervous system.

A yacht with tropical drinks, a game of cards and laughter including the reminder of why the Caribbean has so much exoticism and beauty. The soothing sensation abruptly ended with our guide bellowing, "this is where we should snorkel." He proceeded to do a roll call of all the fish out in these seas and my eyeballs became the size of flying saucers. I heard the B word but tried to act brave and ignore reality, pretending that barracudas were extinct as of yesterday.

"Get in Linda, it's beautiful," shrieked Karen, laughing at me because we discussed my fear of big fish just last night. "We're going to snorkel every day, you wussie. Get in!"

It didn't take long for the underworld to humiliate me. Two minutes underwater, I envisioned a barracuda or other large species coming toward us full speed. I tossed my strategy— barracuda no longer exist—and began flapping around like a zapped lunatic walking on water toward the boat. Karen was on her own. They all laughed insisting that there was no fish larger than my hand down there. Not according to my heart—I was holding it.

Life was gentle in the islands and especially at Jim and Susie's place overlooking Red Hook Bay in St. Thomas. Our luxurious condo was 113 uneven, stone steps—we counted them—down to the white sandy beach and our place in heaven each afternoon as we fried our bodies and skin cancer was dismissed. We wanted to go back to college with a killer tan at all costs. A steep price to pay for our selection of the perfect souvenir.

Transcending into accepting the invitation to indulge in

complete opulence, I was about to become acquainted with a new sensory experience. Food. Fine food. This was going to be the real deal. Like a great artist it was time for a new color on my palette. Associating aroma, beauty of presentation and the burst that ensued allowed my sense of taste to reach a new level of awareness. Learning to appreciate each burst of flavor without the yearning for quantity, this evening's bistro opened my world to a new avenue of exploration. Each course was followed with a sorbet or palette cleanser in order to truthfully imbibe your taste buds for the next presentation. New to me, but my threshold for flavorful food rose to new heights.

"Eat slow my darlings," Jim said to Karen and I.

No desire to cheat myself out of pleasure, the directive became indelible on my soul. An important lesson learned on a trip where we thought the darkest tan was the trophy. How was I going to match these offerings back on campus? New challenges and a remorseful feeling the party was over with food until the real world called.

Music is the universal language through which we all connect; therefore, it was planned into most nights out on the town. We stayed in one evening of our two and half week trip, sadly because we couldn't move from second degree burns on our bodies. Five nights into our high brow vacation and we needed that gritty feeling of outdoor evening excitement—similar to college scenes where the only choice of adult beverages is beer in plastic cups. Red Hook Bay at the dock was serving beer and a calypso band for the locals.

"Yes, we were invited," said Karen's dad. He drove us down there the short distance from the house and gave us money for a cab ride home.

Karen was a temptress with an infectious laugh and rogue glance that always made her that certain kind of beauty who easily connected to people. Tonight the agenda was scoping out the intriguing assortment of "cuties". It didn't take long for her to locate the most attractive guy at the scene. I had a hunch where this was going. The best friendships are defined by reciprocity.

"Lynn, look over there at the two boys—anything?" She loved to flirt so my suggestion was use the cardinal trait of any great heartbreaker—patience. However, the field was competitive with other island beauties so she concocted a plan to spark up a conversation sooner than later.

"Lynn, I'll make you a deal. You go over there and tell him he's caught my eye and I will do the same for you before the trip is over."

Feeling like the queen of the world with nothing to lose I did just that—walked right up to him and delivered the message elegantly, "She likes you."

It worked—imagine that. He held his plastic cup tight with a smirk on his face and a hint of predatory interest—until he saw Karen. Magic occurred unsuspected by either party. He felt like he died and heaven was his for the taking. The other guy was at-best average, but I played the role of happy companion and was promised the same treatment if a similar situation arose. We danced, drank and had the silly notion to take a swim at the dark soft beach with entrusted strangers. Complete bliss and frolicking was the headline of the evening over the fact that Dad might be waiting up for us. Time was not negotiated or really ever considered except in my mind we were stepping over the boundaries. I couldn't confer with Karen she was in another world.

The sun tipped right over the horizon across the water and you didn't need a watch to tell time. We were in trouble.

"Karen! Your Dad is going to kill us!" speaking loud enough to capture her attention just in case she didn't notice the light of day.

"Oh my God, Lynn what are we going to do?" Beside wanting to beat her to a pulp, knowing I was as guilty for not sounding the alarm bell sooner, we scrambled for an idea.

"Let's get in the guy's car and have them drop us off a block from the condo and then think of what we're going to say on the ride." Brilliant plan considering we were busted and the punishment is going to be harsh regardless of any cockamamie plan we could conjure up beyond a miracle.

Sure enough as we approached three blocks away from the condo, there was Kar's dad out doing his morning jog. Irrefutably he wasn't enjoying himself—the look on his face immediately suggested we were bad puppies.

The remainder of the trip was spent looking for Mike-the-Welder at each and every gin mill on the island. Karen was beyond smitten—she thought she loved this guy and wrangled with the idea of not going back to college.

"What? Kar, you can't do this." We had many experiences in high school, but the phase of life we were entering in a very short time, was enriched with bedtime talk of our lives in the real world. This is not how I pictured Karen's future. She was playing out a fantasy in her head and I was untangling this dream of her being a welder's wife on an island. We finally found Mike-the-Welder the last night of our dream vacation (Thank God).

Taking baby steps out to the plane, Karen wept the whole way home.

"That was a fun trip," with a melancholy voice, specifically understating several memories we would never be able to forget. The one trump card to carry me through life was that Karen owed me the same someday. Maybe it would have to be used at 75 years old when I find a cutie in the home. Skinny dipping will not be on the agenda—dismiss the thought. Back to the world of focus and graduating.

4

Reality

B ack to reality including the annoying fact nine credits short of graduation, even with a full load of classes, holds unpleasant thoughts. A swirling mind, a burst of energy for the finish line and dwindling motivation to tackle the tedious work of the last semester, a miracle needed to occur. A plan ensued. Always have a plan and then have a backup plan in case that brilliant idea didn't pan out the way you envisioned. 3 plans on the table can be insurance. Today, the art of persuasion was going to be tested and evaluated.

"Mr. Varney, remember when I worked in the real world this past summer? You know, in the big city I took it upon myself to get a job—key-lining! Well I was wondering if a paper with a dissertation on all the facts and how I accomplished securing a job, the typical work day, etc. would suffice for the 3 elective credits I'm currently short for graduating on time?" Dick Varney was a respected visual communication professor who had worked in the real world and came back to teach—or relax, explaining the situation more realistically.

"Inventive, Linda," he spoke with a wry smile. "Yes, I'll grant you the credits if the paper is awesome and we can use the model at the VAB for future students. Make it stunning!"

Gulp. Really? Cool. The paper, a stunner and plan A worked. Becoming egotistical was also making an about face. Maybe I didn't need to have a plan B—I was getting good at bull-shitting, which is typically categorized as a personality disorder more often than glamorous. Inventive as a bullet point on my resume would be rightfully wrong—this type of thinking is mandatory 8 hours a day on any future job in the art and design genre of the early eighties. There is a fine line between promoting a level of common sense that is an insult to any intelligent person and being transparent and sincere in your convictions. The difference is defined as trust.

The speed of trust was necessary to cross the finish line and complete the final semester like it was meant to be. The biggest test before me is what I didn't envision: the proverbial student who hangs around college hoping to "wrap my mind around the real world want-a-be" while supposedly looking for the big job. This was the last educational chance to show intelligence, knowledge, resourceful behavior and that I was the next legacy of the design world. As my mother would say, "Yeah, Linda's real talented...just ask her."

Shamefully, graduation on time had to include two classes over the summer with the university allowing me to march with my peers in May—and allow my parents all the glory of the big day. Big deal, it was achievable. How hard could that be?

What wasn't factored into the scenario was meeting a geologist over the summer in Lawrence. Falling madly in love with Rick, our relationship developed quickly to the point where most scenes for printability needed to be deleted. Unless Danielle Steele calls, short on minute details for a new series, I would be abstracting them to the point of believability. With life moving quickly, the menacing visual of life on an oil well in the middle of Kansas, scrap-booking as my design outlet, and parents screaming in the background was live theatre in my head. A far cry from three years of elitist images of uber-famous and modestly rich. Something wasn't remotely correct here—the picture perfect life after graduation? Getting the MRS degree was never a goal. Should I shift my thinking? First struggle of the real world and failing was coming up strong—thoughts needed to shift to clever problem-solver status assisting to qualify my answer. A hateful entry into the complex problems of being free to make the tough choices. Proximity to world-class design jobs were realistically in Chicago. Love like I never experienced before was in the here and now including the possibility of the fairy tale. Having it all was part of the equation and at all costs must be attained but how? New bullet points and goals ensued along with sleepless nights and disturbing anxiety.

See how safe school can be and you thought making the grades was so very, very hard?

The summer of 2 classes, unimaginable, deep love and Helen and Billy returned for a visit from Boston with their baby girl who was now 18 months and they were pregnant again. Helen was not the person to ask advice at this point, knowing her opinion on the conundrum between motherhood and career-girl would likely point me in an annoying direction and not solve the real issue. If you can't handle the answer—don't ask. Anxiety rose to levels beyond my wildest imagination. Fleeing the scene made the most sense to improving the odds of landing a solid job with a side order of eccentricity.

Before giving up the ship and leaving the comforts of familiarity, it was time to put in a resume at Hallmark Cards in Kansas City. Hallmark was the go-to job for newbie designers at Kansas University. A comfortable and corporate job that design friends from KU easily obtained. There was a precarious divide between a corporate designer who had to follow every rule and the designer who preferred the unexpected to the boring. In other words, following rules was not a strong suit, but I was willing to fake it for my first job. False. The powers that be at Hallmark noticed I didn't look like Peter Pan in britches. Not being selected to their design team crushed me. It took the better part of one hour to get over the rejection and realize Chicago was the next move forward. The key-lining jobette over the previous summer combined with a fabulous portfolio from the university was a leaping start to finding a job and appear confident and enthusiastic in the face of severe competition. The brutal recession of 1982 took all of us off-guard and the sad reality—I appeared as green as a neon frog in a cheerleader's outfit. Not to mention the "portfolio" was a big black rectangular mass the size of a small sail and it needed to be schlepped from the train to the bus while looking fetching when you walked in the door for an interview—not disheveled.

Living with my parents again was a chore. No job, no money, and my grandma's old Nova for wheels. Rick was a saving grace and his support of continuing the relationship regardless of the geographic challenges made the change bearable for the time being. A job matters in the world especially following four years laboring and ruminating how your life was going to be after the degree was dispensed and firmly planted in your hands. The goal was to sit up straight and act like a goddess with a selection of two pairs of ugly shoes and a disfigured wardrobe that began to appear rustic.

Pounding the pavement for a design job was thee bullet trusting that every other problem would solve itself. Uh huh. How do you flag attention on the crowded expressway to notoriety and prosperity?

"Life without me as your hot-shot designer has the distinct potential of falling into a deep, black hole," words spewing out of my mouth at a point of desperation in the 50th interview. At the very least it caught everyone roaring. Making people laugh was the fang. Years later this line came up at a soiree for the industry and the person who never hired me acknowledged he was remorseful.

"Had to think of something to differentiate myself from the sea of other hires who were lighter shades of green and had prettier clothes. So, why didn't you hire me?"

"I really don't know, dumb move on my part."

In retrospect I must have been uncomfortable to look at and in a boss's world apparently there had to be a worthier selection for a new graphic designer. Maybe a persuasive strategy beyond funny or threatening should be the next bullet point. Imagine you're pontificating on how to be more appealing to the employer. Ask a design guru, and he'll say "hire me to rearrange your portfolio." Seek a career coach and just guessing their quick-fix will be "hire me and you will land the job of your dreams." These were not viable options in light of my financial situation. Great selling tools for them but I needed a new free tool—or basically a miracle. Four months of job seeking and it was February in Chicago, the "hateful month." God doesn't charge much for miracles so I darkened the doorstep of my childhood church. The world didn't lock all doors at this time in history. Without the shameful reminder that everyone at 11:00 am Sunday mass would appear gainfully employed except me, I went during the week while no one was around. Sitting down and staring at the altar, 99% willing to leave my ego at the door, I cried uncontrollably. Tears gushing, pooling on the pew in front of me.

"Please God, what have I done to deserve this frustration and rejection? Wasn't following all the rules except a few bends here and there, what you expected of a college student? If you can show me the light or the problem for what it really is, I promise it will change. Am I being punished for that spring break our junior year in college? The one where I talked Winslow into telling her father she needed an emergency loan for food when in fact the money was being used for an airplane ticket to Fort Lauderdale? I really wanted her to go with me to Karen's dad's well-appointed home on the intercostal with a stocked bar and Cadillac convertible and heated swimming pool. My intentions were innocent. I couldn't fathom leaving her alone in Lawrence, Kansas. Winslow and Karen are the sisters I never had— it would be selfish not to include them in reindeer games. Are you mad at me because the boys on the strip in Fort Lauderdale piled into our convertible full of girls? It was a sin; I know—it's just that I need a job real soon. Oh yeah, and a design job downtown in a swank office preferably with a window," stating high demands all in the same breath.

We were warned in college the first job you land will be short-lived and the typical scenario for designers included changing jobs eight times in four years before you figure out what you want to be for the rest of your life. According to this formula, that puts me deep in the throws of 400 interviews in 4 years—this is not how I pictured the work world. Again, praying for a miracle, the phone rang.

"Linda, we'd like to know if you can come downtown tomorrow for a second interview? This is John Gebhardt with Gebhardt McGuire & Associates, Inc. at 215 W. Superior. Although we've already reviewed your work, could you bring your portfolio with you?" No relation to my last name purely coincidence.

"What time would you like me there?" Not really even remembering who they were in the sea of other firms showing remote interest.

"9 am ok?"

"I can be there at 9." Acting like I had to confer with a packed schedule, secretary and the city of Chicago was seeking my attention on a daily basis, the burst of enthusiasm was macerated and left at the door of my soul. Being an actress is part of the gig and the friction that occurs while appearing important even though you haven't proven a thing. Containing my energy and projecting emphasis on the point the payoff from four years of college may come as early as next week. "Mom, that call was for a second interview."

"Cool. You can take the green limo to the el." The green limo in our house was a reference to the 88 CTA bus which stopped three blocks from our house in the suburb of Park Ridge. Back in the day, the busses in Chicago were a two-toned moss green from the bottom of the windows. The route to work would include a bus, a train and then another train.

"Well, I think I'll drive for the second interview," reminding myself of the horrors of the green limo. "Linda there is no parking down there except for a few lots and it's quite expensive. You might find a few metered spots. Take public transportation." I absolutely hated public transportation. If the train stopped in front of the house and dropped me off at the door of the office, it would have been feasible—but that's not how the system works. Transit in the city was for reaching points of interest not getting to work.

I drove to the interview, received a reasonable starting salary, a glorious window office with a view of the renovation across the street and a parking ticket to the tune of $25.00. Public transportation was $1.50 with transfers. Oops. One problem solved and another was on the horizon—how would I comfortably get to work?

Starting the daily routine with a gnarly stench of urine in the subway, a person singing "Billie Jean" at the top of their lungs in B flat, or the typical scene of someone engaged in a serious conversation with themselves, released a queasy sensation on a good day. You were treated to an involuntary front row seat to the unrehearsed theatre 80% of your calculated time on the train or bus. The popular alternative for most was public transportation or as I liked to refer to them, fixed services. There had to be a better way than handing the car keys over to the bus driver and subway attendants—I didn't like being on someone else's timetable, at least not in this city. Was I developing snob-like traits in light of my new cool job, or was it something different? Overwhelmed with an uncontrollable shaking inside indicating anxiety was visiting again, I began to visualize crusty toothpaste oozing through my muddy brain. Was that it? The train reminded me of the 50 plus interviews and coming up short with a job offer. "I can't do this" surfaced. The star from KU crumbling under the pressure all in a matter of one hour. Oh, God help me, my big moment has arrived and stage fright is trumping a self-assured demeanor. Ah ha—that's why they had us take acting classes in college. Check your posture and attitude and walk straight in the first day like you own the joint. Believe.

Parking the car in a metered spot rationalizing this may

not be a full day, I caved to my first insecurity of the work world. Why not go down and feed the meter—how hard could that be every two hours? Problem solved. Personal mobility and flexibility eased the pain of whatever was ailing me with a non-descriptive itch.

The firm was located in a loft in the up-and-coming River North area several blocks from the perimeter of the loop or downtown Chicago. Years ago these buildings were factories filled with industrial revolution workers carrying silver lunch pails arriving before dawn. Our side of the street was lined with red-brown brick renovations, gutted to the frame, sandblasted inside and out, and fashioned with sleek floor to ceiling windows. "Loft space" was the embraced concept for the artist, dress designer, graphic designer or architect who preferred hip and cool open-style working environments.

Uniting the arts and crafts movement with the emerging age of technology was not really new to those of us who studied the evolution of art, design and the machine in college. Art history was required, uninteresting and frequently became a memorization project abhorred by most design students. Today, the reality of the boring slides and four-inch-thick art history books in lecture hall came to life in a three dimensional visual willingly acting out a character in the scene.

The original loft was a product of the Bauhaus and its solution to the unity of art and technology in one space. Walter Gropius, the founder of the Bauhaus in the 30's, was a genius thinker who could easily visualize the future— talented at anticipating and executing the outcome. God bless him, because we were on the cusp of change and the switch was about to be turned on without an off switch. His vision was spot on. In the modern world of the new century, the open living concept is not trendy it's mandatory.

Across the street from my new office space the facades looked eerily different. One building appeared to be in the throws of a massive renovation and the rest of the block was still tenement housing fashioned from the old factories. Basically they were section 8 slums.

Three blocks north of our artsy district was the Oscar Mayer factory including the delicious waft of toasty lard bathing the wieners every morning at 8:00 am. The Kolling Meat Market was still a thriving anomaly on the near north side in Chicago along with the Cabrini Green housing projects where Division Street met Clybourn Avenue. A dangerous mixture of visuals and smells defining why Chicago will always be a curious city. Neighborhoods didn't always match the neighbors, but somehow everyone managed to get along.

Today was the first official day of my career and living in the moment, beyond being anxiety-riddled, the adrenaline rush reached monumental proportions. Entering the seven story building without a key, you had to proclaim your identity in the vestibule to be buzzed up. Each floor had its own entry by elevator for security purposes. No riff raff. We occupied the sixth floor and shared the building with a dress designer and several high-brow art galleries.

When the speaker asks who it is, should I reply, "It's me. Linda, your new designer. You can all begin now?" Entering the loft, my office was to the left in a corner with a large window looking out at the tenement scene across the street. If you looked to the right a silent, solid view of the John Hancock, Water Tower Place and other significant landmarks consumed the eye. The ceiling went on for miles and most of it was exposed piping and heating and air conditioning ducts. The ambient light was natural daylight. Our drawing tables were fashioned with cool task lighting that wiggled around like a stiff hose and was able to directly hit our focus area on the art board with precision similar to a surgeon. The other illumination, for show mostly, was track lighting from the Italians around the corner who just unloaded the boat with the newest concept in overhead lights. Small escutcheons supporting a horizontal pole and a thread-thin wire hung straight down with a bulb on the end. If the Italians hadn't sold them the entire story of the latest and greatest European invention on American soil, I would have thought the lights were scrounged up from the old tenement building across the street.

"Focus on your new career, Linda and act smart even when you're in complete bewilderment of what's in front of you."

The best designers admit to owning baby-brains that still had a corner of their cerebral cortex in complete wonderment. Like a child's mind whose existence is slowly making way for reality, similar to the obscure formulation of where the goldfish goes when its flushed down the toilet. Children may ask, "When grandpa dies are we going to flush him down the toilet?" Where things go when they are not black and white and right in front of us makes us frazzled—unzipped, but also defines why we prefer the conceptual age to the information age. I knew this livelihood struck the balance between fine art and rigid design. Unfortunately, it can take an entire career to wrap your head around where you fit in the picture—I didn't have that long—I demanded everything right now.

Artists in this era of the early 80s could live comfortably with the notion that anything can happen in the process with an outcome that wasn't exact. No. No. Designer's had an insatiable desire to control the entire process including watching the finished product roll off the press. Interpreting the beginning of the project, we needed to know everything about the human race, space, medicine, engineering, food science, cosmetics, orange juice, filtered water (bottled water was not in vogue in the 80s, the B52s were). In other words, we had to be braniacs with a visual solution that migrated from cerebral parts unknown. If you wanted to compete, you better do your homework and the accompanying exercises.

We sketched until our fingers were raw. A great designer didn't begin to formulate ideas until they thoroughly read and macerated the copy from the client like vested partners in the business we're promoting. You were required to offer a unique interpretation to the project without being branded a weirdo. A refined eccentric was ok as long as you bathed and wore black and white, the uniform of a designer. Otherwise, stick with Ann Taylor and the Gap for lack of another style. Do not go visit the client like you slept in your clothes. It was time to own an iron. Do not use dippity-do as it produced helmet-hair and this was a serious telltale differentiating a good designer from a want-a-be.

My head was about to pop off. All this new information was boot camp training. I was being taught the ropes by the best. Always work for the best—not like I had a choice but it is a great rule to follow if you're lucky. At this point in my life, looking back at the ripe old age of 22, I was lucky more times than not.

My boss, John Gebhardt, had the aura of a quintessential graphic designer of the era with a chiseled dignified face similar to John F. Kennedy. His style emoted a gracious smile stretching ear to ear, ensuring a comfort zone that was most inviting. He worked hard, had great ideas and deserved the next step forward in his career not to mention it was high on his to-do list. The firm hired me as a newbie from KU with an inventive Bauhaus style combined with an insatiable desire to be seated at the adult table. John made it a point to train me to compete with the big boys and mentor exactly how it's done.

The first week on the job was slow. Thank God. I fussed about the cubicle organizing my tools and indulging in liquid lunches with the bosses at the Thai restaurant around the corner, learning the fine art of eating with chopsticks. Before the first week on the job, I didn't know a chopstick from a candlestick, however it was obvious being in tune with culture, food and art was enormously important for success. My sentiments: put me down, I'm in love with all of it and willing to explore all the mysteries hidden in this city.

Week two of my career and a tidal wave of projects came rushing through the door. Is this how it works? You sharpen pencils for a week and then ask for forgiveness and the right to breathe the next. Yep. A busy shop is a happy shop and when the white horses deliver work, you smile and rise to the occasion. The first assignment was an enormous 148-page catalog for WilsonJones, an office product company, complete with the highest order of organizational skills necessary to send the book to print with nary a mistake. Now I know where the anxiety itch was coming from—fear of failure—the stage was set to produce a flawless project. My obligation was to smile, pay attention, read a ruler correctly and not break a sweat or the budget. My role morphed into keeping track of little detailed parts to the whole, and not appear stupid in the eyes of anyone in the office or the client. Scheduling photo shoots, ordering galleys of type (specifying type by hand), designing a color coding system for each of their product lines, figuring out the importance of the size of type for heads and subheads and, of course, during this lengthy process, please do not make a mistake. Three weeks turned into two months learning the typical large project always had extensions to the deadline. You could bury this formula in your head to ease the pain of pressure. Good thing I had all the pencils sharpened.

Mixed in with the chaos you were handed a logo to design, an ad to create and potentially another visual communication project waiting in the wings always with an important reminder that mistakes cost money. Why was all this glamorous? Because you received a paycheck every two weeks. No work—no paycheck.

And, one other very important aspect of being 22 with a degree and a job—time to move into my own apartment.

While it's nice living with parents during all these horrific deadlines, working 10 to 12 hour days—saving money for a deposit on a big-girl apartment was a desirable goal. The tasks of responsibility loomed ever-larger actually rescinding the anxiety of "life". Funny how that works. The purity of the message: looking for a job is more stressful than having a job and a step closer to proving your authenticity. Hurrah!

My high school friends shared the same boat. Receiving their first official title beyond student, we were all figuring out how to leave mommie and daddie. Karen and I decided, best friends for 12 years, we should move out together and get our first apartment. Pining for downtown or Lincoln Park, Karen was afraid of the city so we compromised and lived in a complex in Chicago close to Park Ridge, our hometown. It was still far enough away to keep mom and dad from checking in on us. Karen's dad had the whole place furnished because one of his condos had recently sold. Perfect. Living large, the place was beautiful and ready for entertaining.

October 1, 1983 was the beginning of my responsible life and I was Madame Full-Charge, until the first harsh bite of reality hit, rent was due and my car was on its last leg. Luckily, my parents let me take my fake, French provincial bedroom set bought new when I was eleven. Insisting I include the canvas canopy of the single bed, the scene was worthy of laughter after Karen and I decided— it's not cool to have a ruffled, canopy bed and a rock-star design job downtown. They don't match.

I didn't necessarily need a car since the train was within walking distance. Uh huh. The transportation issues lurked and morphed into a nagging problem. Long hours at the office and unpredictable places that needed to be visited during the day lent itself to driving into the city for work. Keeping a car downtown and feeding the meter or parking in a lot was becoming expensive—including racking up unpaid parking tickets. It was my way of pledging allegiance to a job that required you to be mobile and in control. Look smooth, fetching and be prepared to visit the client, the library, the photographer or possibly the typesetting house at any given moment.

Youth is so wonderful—nothing annoys you as long as you're bathed in compliments, receive a decent paycheck and enjoy weekends with friends and significant others. Money soothes the nerves and liquor enhances the effect.

Working at GMA was now approaching eighteen months along with conceit, the self-assured demeanor from college and an enkindled desire to not only design for clients, but succumb to the unwritten idea that notorious designers cull their craft for other designers with the reward of winning numerous awards and appearing in books that give a nod to your greatness. This is how things worked in our world. Money and not living the life of a starving artist was simply not enough. We always wanted more—personally enjoying the front of the line when they pass out opportunity.

5

....

Reality

Surrendering control to others is not the best way to start the day—ever. If you want the carrot, be hungry. I found myself famished and willing to do what it takes to keep my place in line. It was the fall of 1984—mergers and acquisitions were fashionable for corporations in America who wanted to rule the world and devour poorly run companies suffering from the repercussions of the recession of the early 80's.

John Gebhardt, specifically, became the third firm selected for comprehensively submitting ideas for a new magazine to be launched by a corporation held secret and privy to only those working on the submissions. The storyboards included several cover designs and three interior spreads. Clues were limited and shrouded in secrecy. Who were the other 2 design firms in this competition? You didn't need incendiary music to figure out something big was on the horizon.

"Linda, I personally need your input and design ideas," John point blank confides, prepping me for long nights and weekends. "The rewards could be huge. Beatrice (oops he told me), is going to be the largest conglomerate corporation in America. This magazine we're doing will represent many of the national and international food companies brought under one corporation. I need you and your talent and undivided attention."

"Will I be involved in the client presentation or just part of the crazy and frenetic environment around here leading up to the reveal?" I asked being the intrepid explorer trying to visualize glory and fame before the first idea was even put to paper. John knew I was on the same page when describing design ideas and how to begin the process. Design is not a decoration. Whatever came out of this office had to convey that message. I decided to write it on the walls—we could paint them later.

See what happens when you work hard, make a few mistakes and carry a leadership quality that cultivates a strong mind? Being a designer brought down to the lowest common denominator was a fancy name for a problem solver. You never apologize for the work that you produce—it's of the highest left directed thinking out there. It becomes an addiction, for most, to spew out problems with glee—if you want to rise above that theory and become a worthwhile leader, reach for the solution first and work backwards from there with expert deductive reasoning skills. Works like a charm—most of the time.

Not to mention, being at the right place at the right time helps. Enamored that at almost 24 years old, the opportunity to deliver the performance of a lifetime was right in front of my face. Time to transmit emotions through words and visuals—and win the client over.

The task at hand was transforming the predictable corporate magazine into a chariot of grandiose value. Churning ideas initially thought to be hot, suddenly turned cold—typical of the process. We needed to think futuristic and differentiation as this magazine would be Beatrice Food's tool to opening new markets worldwide. No small task. We were wizards full of magical powers with a superstar team of creative athletes. No wussies and whiners as we gathered ideas and pontificated as to their relevance.

Bottom line, we won...fair and square. Hard, dedicated toiling within a team that grew to wealth and fame and additional projects elevating us to premier design firm status in Chicago. Exuberant designers, photographers, printers and writers lined up to work with us—we were the flavor of the month. Instead of working through the night to get the line perfectly straight for the client's approval, I was looking over the shoulder of a new team making sure they followed my specific directions to the finite degree—in a matter of a few short years. My salary tripled, I became a partner and received a little red sports car as a bonus—probably for not whining through the journey.

The conquest and flurry of effervescence has a very short

memory. The chase, the big win and the adrenaline rush of victory when a project goes well and the check clears, includes the clean sweep turning into the dirty depression of exhaustion. It was part of the game and you needed to get used to the feeling without doping yourself up with fancy meds or liquor.

As a team, the goal was to fulfill the demand of new projects coming from different divisions within the new conglomerate called Beatrice Foods. We delivered a great product, creating demand for our firm—now we needed to complete the tripod necessary for success—fulfilling the demand. In other words, it is essential to hire a crack staff and notch up the leadership skills.

Beatrice went public shortly after the magazine released; the work continued at a feverish pace. The adrenaline flow never stopped including large photo shoots in LA with actors and actresses and big-name directors who bathed us in praise. This steady stream of consistent work and high-brow accolades continued for two more years until the party got stale and the greed of corporate America reared its ugly head:

In 1986, Beatrice became the target of leveraged buyout specialists Kohlberg Kravis Roberts. They ultimately took over the firm for US$8.7 billion — at the time the largest leveraged buyout in history — and over the next four years sold it off, division by division. Its smaller international food operations were sold to Reginald Lewis, a corporate attorney, creating TLC Beatrice International in 1987, becoming the largest business in America run by an African American and the first company to reach a billion dollars in sales, with a black man at its head. In 1990, the last of Beatrice's assets were sold to ConAgra Foods. Most of Beatrice's brand names still exist, but under various other owners, as trademarks and product lines were sold separately to the highest bidder.

By late 1987, most of the large projects had dried up for the firm and we were left with not much new work since it became impossible to replace the volume—too busy working. It was time for me to move on. Almost five years working for the same company, different structure and a pension for magazine design alerted the next step in the career progression. At this point, interviewing was all new to me again. Loathing the process, at least I didn't look like a frog and was equipped with presentable clothes and sensible shoes.

The angst of being out on the streets again hung over my head. What really hung over my head and prompted the sensible shoes was the repercussions of a high-horse idea I didn't need to pay for parking tickets. In my little big mind those orange stickers on my car were reminders to not park on the sidewalk. That's not the way Daley, the mayor of Chicago, saw it. He wanted his $16,000 I racked up over the course of all these years including late fees. The car wasn't even worth $16,000. It was revenue for the city and the mayor wanted his money. No More Scofflaws We're Coming After You—the headline read in the newspaper. Geez. What a windfall for the city since none of us villains took the ticket seriously. Therefore, I purchased sensible shoes for hoofing it on the bus and train, again. Was it laziness (couldn't be that lazy after working for 5 years straight, 10 hour days without complaining) or something else beyond the nefarious smell of public transportation? Impatience was high on the list of suspects.

The big black sail, or portfolio turned into a neat presentation a quarter of its original size. I had bragging rights, however, logically no amount of preening will compensate for a mediocre compendium of your work. No worries, interview with someone who believes they are ridiculously more talented than you and likely you'll receive a comprehensive analysis of your presentation. No charge. Look at the bright side, it cost you a little humility and in return your peer's ego donated more than they probably should have, but glowed as the door shut and they immersed themselves in three days of self-importance. Your good fortune was listening carefully and heeding the criticism knowing it is a disparaging trait to own but pays off in big dividends if executed correctly. Consider it practice and no one is above listening to what another human being has to say.

Envisioning the future, the outcome appeared to hinge on two questions: "What do you want to do?" A luxurious position considering the success of the past five years assured me a meaningful job. The other side of the hinge begged the question: "What one thing is missing to achieve total happiness?" No fibbing, it pointed directly at being a mommy.

Obviously, the struggle ensuing was how to fuse the prodigious role of motherhood with continuing the constant motion of the gerbil wheel required to stay in a fast-track career. The solution meant burying the conflict, hoping the subconscious mind would assist the conscious mind into making great decisions from this day forward and all roads would meet on the yellow-brick road. You are not in Kansas anymore, Linda.

Living day to day is a mantra if you're a hippie relying on grass clippings for food. There are a lot of restrictions placed on "having it all", not to mention I've heard it's a playground for your demons. Focus required mental discipline including an EQ and an IQ high enough for reasonable success. Both sides of the cerebral circuitry needed to be in perfect symphony. So far, I haven't demonstrated this pursuit, considering the nagging reality of unpaid parking tickets exposed I was flawed somewhere.

Defects reveal change is necessary. Doing the same thing over and over again with similar results, falls under the stupid column. Resistance to change can be the choke-hold allowing the gate to close on respect and distinction. It was time to change my habits of impatience and take the train. The train would give me time to think about the EQ + IQ equation and my shortcomings. I had a resolve to position everything exactly right for having it all.

By now, I was living in a three-story, walk-up greystone in Lincoln Park. Ironically, the el (train in any other city beside Chicago) stopped at the end of my block. As my mother liked to remind me, "You practically have to fall out of bed and you're on the train." Gulp, she's right.

The city had settled with the scofflaw idiots, including me, and all criminals set up with a payment plan and forgiven for 40% of the fines. Now a reformed park-a-holic, tormenting me was the lingering question of why it was hard to board these vessels. Promising myself the answer would come to me in a form that was not obvious—there were other things deserving of my attention including putting the two questions mulling around in my head of how to bring together a career and motherhood seamlessly.

Having it all, was a fashionable subject for casual conversation because everyone had an opinion. The 80s and 90s found women declaring their right to have both. I wasn't convinced this empirical formula worked. Can you rub your belly in a circular motion while simultaneously patting the top of your head and keep the motion going perfectly for ten minutes? Try it. The only people I know that can pull off this maneuver, successfully, are drummers and people in circus acts. Our brains aren't typically set up this way. Therefore, unless we have two brains installed, odds have it the triumph of having it all is just an illusion. You can fake it, pretend and exclaim you are the 5% of society of woman that hit career/motherhood full-on and still breathe air without assistance, but the secret of this success was elusive. The 5% weren't fessing up to the unclean spirit they fought with each night. Or was I wrong in my assumptions?

A swirling mind can set you off like a top spinning toward the edge. A better position was to live in the present setting aside a day for rumination. Enjoy good fortune and find a job that worked for the here and now. A little money in the bank helped, but at 28 I was sucked in to wanting more of what I just had.

Offered a senior graphic design position at a prestigious design firm that needed an organized thinker to manage a large banking client, I easily replied, "Yeah, I can do that."

The pay was great, the other senior designers were about the same age—reaching for stardom and a fatter wallet. The only trap was similar to the last job. The paradigm was consistent—if the client goes away so do you unless you are colossal at researching and landing new clients. I wasn't even remotely sure how to attempt the first call for new work. My buddies at this design firm weren't willing to show me either—I was a woman and it was traditionally a boy's club environment. If you landed a client worthy of keeping yourself in a job, the threat to any design firm was that you would start your own company and take the client. Fair enough, now what?

Popping from job to job was not ideal, therefore I engaged in very serious thought to select a trajectory extrapolating from the past six years in the industry. Surfacing was the need for a strategy on how to compartmentalize and utilize the memories of what transpired in these short years.

It's worth more than any good book out there on the subject, to sit for a day and engage in a thought process recalling some of the highlights. In contrast to your egofest, aim to recall events not-so-glamorous. This exercise moderates the brain and the soul shoring up the foundation necessary to add the next story.

For me, patterns emerged and enlightened my soul. Listening to yourself and the advice of others is rhetoric, the true gift is how to be your own crow-keeper with all this information. Developing an innate sense of what to discard and what to include for forward momentum is a fine art better defined as mind control. Dismiss the demons who love to come out to play on a day dedicated to rumination, identify them by name and give them a good, swift kick in the ass. This exercise is perfunctory to growth. I designated myself a sophomore, figuring the hardest lessons were yet to come. Now it was time to examine the next step in employment—again.

The Beatrice account and enormous dedication to the craft of producing a magazine brought about many favorite memories. Enamored with all the little details and crushing responsibility of meeting expectations includes the erotic sensation uncertainty emits. No one ever died meeting deadlines in this business, but the heightened frenzy between the corporate executives and anyone else on the hook for a bungled completion date, you'd think we worked in an emergency room's triage center. Even the nagging, curious memories are ones I simply can't forget.[3]

6

Learning to Win
with Grace

If you need to remind yourself of why *just do it*, is such a popular phrase with deep-seeded meaning this scene may help:

Cousin Eddie, at least eight years my senior, was a corporate man and I respected and trusted him and his lovely wife. Our Grandma's car, my main vehicle of transport, died. I needed a car and at this point in my career, a used one would suffice. Eddie owned and was about to sell his VW, orange-colored bug, and I was the eager buyer willing to listen to its problems trusting Eddie. I'll drive this car until something better comes along.

"Linda, the only problem with this car is that the passenger's side floorboard has a rust spot and it kind of leaks. It will need to be fixed before the whole bottom drops out on that side." Fair enough, I'd find some time to have it looked at—time being the inoperative word.

"How long do you think I have?" with that look of procrastination knowing the only choice was to wait until the last minute.

"Don't wait too long!" Insisting that listening was in my best interest with a gentle reminder Cousin Eddie was not a mechanic he was a corporate executive.

"What do you think? Couple of weeks?" I asked pushing for the last possible date before disaster struck, knowing the Beatrice magazine was currently deep in the throes of a crucial deadline and meandering around town looking for a used car was not on the to-do list—at all.

Of course, during deadlines, I made the decision to drive downtown and put my ratty little VW bug in a lot. Wise thinking knowing anything can happen at press time. Always be prepared. Sure enough, on this rainy spring day, the call came in to the office that the printer needed an approval on a sensitive subject in the magazine before they went to final print.

"Linda, I need you to go to 2 N. LaSalle, pick up Pat, and

drive her over to the printers so she can put the final approval on this part of the magazine," John said pointing to a world-wide issue and I was the messenger. "And, by the way, that means right this very second." Time was of the essence and Pat was the full description of a high-level, female corporate executive. A senior marketing manager capable of making breakthrough decisions on the spot.

"What about my car? It's such a ratty vehicle," expressing concern when the obvious point was the time frame and cars didn't matter—a decision was necessary and within the next half hour.

Jumping into my car, throwing empty soda cans into the back seat and pleasing up the passenger side, my panic was real. The hole in the passenger side was real too! Hmm. We can't have things both ways in this world. If you want service, you get what you get—no matter what level you are on. The peons (me) will be servicing the upper level elitist on this rainy day from hell. Smile.

"Pat, excuse my car, we all know the deadline is the fiduciary responsibility at this very moment. We'll get this taken care of."

"Linda, I am enamored with your ability to rise to the occasion and expedite this in a most unusual manner." Oh thank God, thinking to myself being ultra-embarrassed.

As we rounded the corner downtown, the rain came in the form of a downpour including puddles the size of a small pond. The VW bug found an unavoidable puddle, and rainwater streamed through the small hole in the floorboard like a wake from a waterski, giving Pat an enema and her perfect clothes a lovely shade of city-grey including the smell of sewer residue.

An ugly scene, "Linda this isn't your fault," Pat graciously concluded. We did complete the mission and my pride was reduced to rubble. Angry I was put in the position of such embarrassment, a whimper of hope rose from the awkward scene. Someone noticed I did what it took to get the job done. Two weeks later, as soon as the magazine received nods, accolades and our check arrived, I was surprised with an $8,000 deposit on my new red Honda Prelude with all the upgrades. Best part of the whole incident—a laughing point for anyone willing to listen to the story. Be patient, if you do the right thing someone is likely to act profoundly if you don't whine too loud. It was this experience that taught me courage and the lesson that predictability does not really exist. Enumerating my good points and reflecting on the failures, I concluded magazine design and art direction appeared stable and I thoroughly loved the discipline.

My lucky star was bright and a connection was made in an unconventional manner.

Living at 1037 W. Wellington and all the colorful adventures of having a great apartment with roommates that got married and moved out to all the people who were lined up to move into this apartment due to location, size and price, it was a golden era of 9 years. In 1988 when I had an open bedroom at the apartment and did not want to move, I took a chance and placed an ad in Roommates Chicago. One of the pivotal and great moments of my career occurred when I found a woman, and new roommate, moving from Canada because she was to become the new *Outside Magazine* art director.

After 4 months (magazine turnover is huge), she told me she was moving back to Canada and the publisher would be looking for an interim art director because the assistant art director was simultaneously leaving. "This is a volatile environment Linda, however, if you do some layouts and redesign pages, they would consider you even though you don't have consumer magazine experience." That's exactly what occurred. Redesigned a few spreads, gave them my typographical and art director points of view and was hired immediately on a contract basis. I love having an audience to present my strong point of view—the results never fail.

A glorious job, playing with type, art directing photos and fine art from all over the world and learning more about photography through the eyes of famous photographers. An enviable job from anybody looking in, I was deep in the throes of working diligently while looking over my shoulder as the publisher sought out his new Executive Art Director. Apparently, without the consumer magazine experience necessary for the ferocious environment of competition on all levels in this industry, I was a substitute for the real deal. Yes, I was part of the egos on a daily basis, feeling as though I was cushioned and allowed to do my work and the powers that be decided not to involve me in the nefarious politics. Perfect. My goal was to ensconce myself in a tiny office with thousands of professional photos and art submitted to the hottest magazine emerging in the sporting arena including information on outdoor activities in inconspicuous places dotting the world map. The editor was a pure brainiac by the exact definition, and if this was a temporary position my head became a sponge veraciously storing each particle. Lessons In "Just Do It" boldly displayed in his office included an 8 ft. x 8 ft. sign from Nike plastered on the wall. Included in the message, the invisible sign; do not disturb me or ask a question unless you absolutely do not know how to answer the question yourself. Only smart people work here—heed the warning. Another work environment requiring the circuitry of the brain to hit on all cylinders. Wishing the job would never end and they would recognize my talent and excuse the lack of experience, my luck ran out. What did materialize was far more exciting and alluring.

The future is always ripe for discovery—existing by this theory. My brain was on fire, and my spirit grew proportionately. Thrilled to be invited on a white-water rafting on the Cheat and New Rivers in West Virginia with a friend, a rare coincidence in my young life of art meeting life exposing the unspoiled wilderness only seen through the slides of photographers. Three weeks earlier designing spreads at the magazine specifically focusing on kayaking tournaments on the New River, I envisioned a frontier outpost and today I was hitching a ride to pure adventure. The side dish—girl meets boy.

Keith and I were assigned to drive in a car together—there were at least 7 vehicles in a caravan from Chicago to Charleston, West Virginia. Fiddling about with the music in the car, using the knob as an obvious distraction to the conversation ensuing, I felt a comfortable tension building.

"You are an art director?" Is that similar to a graphic designer?" Keith asks breaking the stiffness of the spring air with the most complex question asked every day of my profession.

Conspicuously using an indirect approach, opening the floor with, "the descriptions aren't all that different." Not wanting to appear aloof, yet curious to where this conversation was going, the next 100 miles included a complete and open discussion on the differences and similarities associated with the two interchangeable titles. An interesting observation, while cocooned in the car for hours, Keith's ability to pause before he spoke. Not a trait I possessed, but it was admirable and remarkable. Someone who chooses their words carefully, makes me feel emotionally safe. Learning from past relationships which nerves are unwittingly being stepped on.

Long sentences of career and jobs and choices in life heightened a growing attraction including a predictable emotional attachment. For every 10 words he spoke, I could easily add 100. I was type A personality and concluded Keith was somewhere between a B and a C.

I'd never been to West Virginia and for that matter camped on a river's edge in the wilderness. Or, camped other than the Girl Scout weekends which were hateful because it always seemed to rain and my mind could not wrap around sleeping on the ground; I liked my snuggly bed. What was the point? I opted to not display my strain with the sleeping arrangements. What did capture my attention and growing attraction to Keith was his sunny invitation to learn how to sleep outside and keep life simple. Inordinate excess always tempted new and glorified designers—it was soothing to watch the simplicity of pure fun with a few props like a ball and loads of accompanying laughter. Nighttime activities around a campfire were the fulcrum enabling each personality to enlighten us in their stories and songs. The triumph existed in who could make us laugh the loudest; the kind of hilarity you almost beg to stop because your stomach hurts.

Imagine work being predominantly your focus and on this Memorial Day weekend in West Virginia, the pivotal positive change rerouting my entire existence was underway. Still working at *Outside Magazine*, you would have thought I was a celebrity. The trip included over 30 friends of friends who each shared an enthusiasm for outdoor activities and I currently worked at the most widely read magazine on the market for adventure seeking humans. Distracting me from the impending release from the magazine once their new art director took over, having a boyfriend and the frenetic pitch of nothing else matters in the world was worth the excruciating reminder that I would be seeking new employment, again, within a few weeks.

However, *Outside Magazine* wasn't willing to dispose of me without a parting gift. Or two. Never really establishing whom at the magazine was directly responsible for the connection, I received a call while still employed and only three days left on the job.

"Linda, we would like to interview you for the position of Executive Art Director for J. Crew's catalog," spoke the voice on the other line. "*Outside Magazine* thinks highly of your talent and you might be a perfect fit for the direction we are taking this catalog."

At the time of my tenure at *Outside*, the magazine was in the process of a complete redesign and my point of view in establishing a lifestyle look with friendly type and cutting copy to its absolute minimum became noteworthy. This strong perspective was not popular among the editors who believed copy was more important than art. J. Crew wanted a free, lifestyle ambience with the most minimal of copy to express their product. Mail order catalogs were associated with the Sears Roebuck style and this was about to change—catalogs were filling the mailboxes and J. Crew's mission was to be the popular and first choice.

Today, selectively befitting their first choice in making this dream happen, included a plane ride to New York City, a limo waiting at JFK, a tour of the city and lunch at their headquarters at 57th Street. Yet, something did not quite feel right. Realizing, falling victim to unnamed anxiety was typical from past interviews, it just couldn't be ignored. Soaring the skies of greatness, aware that this moment only comes once in a lifetime, I desperately opened myself up to joy and living the dream.

"Linda, you are perfect for this position. We are reorganizing the whole company to introduce a lifestyle feel to our mail-order catalogs. Our designers are completing a new line of clothing and we want you to be on our team developing the cutting edge in casual wear portraying our image on these pages in the catalog."

My eyes began to glaze over with an accompanying pulse ready to explode at any fleeting moment. They might as well have said, "Linda we are going to dress you up like a princess in our new casual wear line and ride you through the streets of Manhattan on a unicorn." It would have all sounded exactly the same.

The non-descriptive itch returned, and I wanted to jump

out the 13th story window—now! Keeping my cool and letting my soul simmer to a boil, I woke up and listened to the offer. These moments in time are the litmus test judging the value of how high your EQ and IQ combine to assist you in displaying a gracious demeanor. Telling yourself to vomit in private—not while the committee is watching and taking notes. I puked in the bathroom—the Chinese noodles from lunch were in their original form. What a wussie, but the good news: no one knew—what a pro.

A generous offer including all the perks an Executive Art Director in New York City could imagine—paid trips back to Chicago to see family and friends (all well and good if the time was available). This title had numerous attachments of promise and I knew better than to take it all at face value. I would be trapped in NYC working 10-12 hour days at least 6 days a week for the better part of two years.

On the 2 hour return trip to Chicago I asked for serenity, divine intervention in assisting my decision and two blankets from the flight attendant. I didn't want anyone on the plane to know I was in crisis—like it even mattered.

7

Reminders of Luck

The missing link dawned on me and the true meaning of success wasn't the money, the new car and its addictive smell, or the fame and freedom. Those jewels were rewards. Looking back, I employed bullet points in order to reach the goal: graduating. Currently flailing aimlessly in a sea of whatever, I needed to synthesize the past six years and develop a new self concept of what the next six years looked like. Visuals of dating and potentially finding the one, traveling, excitement of living in a vibrant city combined with a spirited attitude were the basic elements and sources of inspiration sitting at the new drawing table of life.

Creative visualization was required to set new goals allowing my future self to talk back and assist in decision's like the gargantuan one I was standing on the edge of during this moment in time. A dangerous strategy unless I could faithfully visualize who this person is. Broad narratives of intent are hollow and potentially fleeting. The fuzzy visual needed to be a paint-by-number in my mind with more of the exact colors filled in for definition. The discovery suggested using all my resources, talent and experience to support a worthy cause and message: I wanted to be a mom and time was running out.

Awaiting me on the arrival runway was no job and a leap of faith that employment in Chicago would most certainly crop up and the new excitement of a boyfriend and new friends will fill in the blank feeling.

Excruciatingly, I called to decline the position. A turning point in my life and an agonizing way to proceed resisting the urge to visualize what could have been a glorious reward of fame and potential riches. Not wanting to view the decision as a concession, the gamble paid off and my love life and social life reached a feverish pitch. I found Keith. And, Keith found me. Our attraction was our brilliance and the collection of friends who shared the same direction.

Our first date was to the Cubby Bear across from Wrigley

Field to see the Tom Tom Club. A night to remember with a match made in heaven—we both loved the city and were explorers of everything Chicago had to offer. Likewise, his friends would become lifelong buddies of mine as we all proceeded to enjoy the changes Chicago was experiencing in this genre. Neighborhoods were gentrifying and the newest term to hit the waves: yuppies. Young urban professionals. This new journey extinguished all resentment for a life that could have been; an isolated existence of living in terrifying silence when the work day ended in New York City.

The coolest news to date inserted the fact I still had the swag. Chicago Magazine wanted me. Imagine that. They even put together a job description combining my promotional background with art directing lead features in a national magazine.

The good news—the realization I wasn't launching a career, it felt more like falling deep in the throes of a great ride. The bad news was turning 30 and feeling like the youngest set of zealots were graduating and anxious to take over my reigns, like sand through a sieve. Predictably, this vision is loss of energy and the will to compete. Never was my mantra. The newest goal was to add higher octane to my think tank and rev it up like a little girl who had her training wheels removed.

At 30, we were on a roll. Keith worked as an industrial designer and really liked the discipline of what he saw in the term graphic designer. One common goal equal to both of us was succumbing to the risk adverse nature of starting a business most people our age loathed. For that matter anyone under pressure to perform in this business, where most outcomes are out of one's control, the pinnacle of success is the monetary reward plus the freedom. More likely for me, the itch of autonomy and self-direction combined with a desire to chart my own course while visuals of babies danced in my head. Tucked away in parts unknown included solving the mystery of whether the combination of career and motherhood was achievable. The curiosity factor was worthy of encountering roadblocks of dangers and promises of a prosperous future along the journey. Lurking between these polar ideas was a visual of sharing my talent with offspring. Sometimes wondering if I played a game with myself to defeat the notion that having it all was a chimerical plan.

Chicago Magazine offered the hands-on entry into the world of computers along with a mandate insisting each employee needed to be on-board with the system in 6 months, better known today as desktop publishing.

"How is this better than what we do now?" Same question every art director, graphic designer and typesetter asked. I thought a computer was a big box the size of a refrigerator and if you wanted to experiment be prepared for the box to explode because you were not the equal of the mathematical genius you envisioned the computer scientist who wore plaid suits. Turning it on might break the box. Working at the high profile design firm two years ago a Mac was brought in like a newborn baby too young to hold. We played around with one of the first Apple Mac's off the assembly line—a Macintosh II. The screen bit mapped the type and images.

I would have rather swallowed paper whole than let anyone tell me the computer would replace everything we were taught up to this point in time. Too bad, it was shoved down our throats at *Chicago Magazine* and you better embrace all its features. Not to mention be up to speed when we take the conventional method and throw it out the window. A radical movement meant I could let the words ring sanitized or change. If I pause to reflect on the experience of learning how to compute art, it was pure misery. A necessary evil and like it or not there was no turning back. Happy the magazine was generous in their offering to teach the creatives while we worked and collected a paycheck.

When fear creeps inside the inquisitive brain we all run

for the door discovering emptiness on the other side. This sensation is better known as change. The fear of change is the unknown. Can I make it? What's it? It is thinking in a way our brain's circuitry has never done before. Learning to make the crossover from hand to eye coordination of yesterday's art world, tomorrow meant producing an oblique object directly from the box in front of you—the computer. Huh? My world was turning cruel simply because this whole computer thing was a seismic shift. The fear existed in realizing I was back at square one, reevaluating my career and whether I was smart enough to keep up with the changes. Our brains do mysterious things to our senses under challenging situations.

"Listen up Linda," I repeated to myself, "or become a waitress."

Ironically, at this point, *Chicago Magazine* was a pay-cut and waitressing was looking lucrative.

Keith was more of the methodical mind and helped me shape a future with priorities that made sense.

"We need to buy a MAC and learn. On our own time." He concluded with earnest and without looking back, that's what we did.

I was particularly enamored with its new plastic smell, silently hoping there were no directions as I liked to dive right in and proceed; press a button and things would magically happen. Like an established tree in a dark forest it felt similar to fighting for sunlight as everything surrounding you is growing rapidly. In order to survive, those with the strongest base were going to wallow through the learning curve and the rest would die. I made the commitment to learn—at my pace.

Chicago Magazine didn't see my point of view and dismissed me. Replacing the 30 year olds with a younger version of myself who enjoyed Mr. Computer. Towing the line of optimism, I believed there was another opportunity out there worthy of my attention. Scotch-taping my resume together, *Playboy Magazine* was interested in my talents. The build of a thirteen-year-old girl entering puberty, I knew it wasn't my body they desired. Curious as to what an art director does all day at the famous institution designed around men's secretive desires, I walked into the offices and everyone stared toward my direction. "They can't possibly be looking at my body," thinking to myself sheepishly bowing my head resisting the urge to stare back.

The interview was relatively brief with a job description similar to someone who orders art for the "literature features" in the magazine. In other words, a boring job with a fancy title and a lot of inquisitive people asking questions I'd probably have fun making up lies to, for my own amusement.

The next call was to the *Chicago Tribune*. Through the art world Grapevine there was a temporary position for an art director leading the Books' section, Your Place (real estate), and Food section. I was all in on this job believing after six months it would lead to exciting avenues sure to entice my curious side of being.

"The current art director will be going on a 6 month leave of absence due to medical reasons," the Creative Director discussed. Hmm.

What kind of medical issues roamed around in my mind? Learning over the years to keep my mouth shut and put the parking brake on, I took a chance and accepted the job without initiating any negative rhetoric possibly leading to a dark place. The pay was the most I had made in a long time. The risk was worth it because this world-renowned paper combined old-fashioned art direction with the computer. Perfect.

Wasting time on learning and simultaneously producing a product proved to be the nemesis of any corporation attached to the bottom line, and my sanity. Keith and I were trying to figure out where our place in line for success existed in the current revolution. Tinkering with the computer as a tool in the comfort of my own home, while working for a paycheck ensured I wouldn't be a threat to society.

The *Chicago Tribune* was the bomb! Creative, easy work, high pay and if my work was complete, I could go home—some days I left at 1pm. The situation set Keith and I up for learning the computer. By this time, as a couple we were seriously falling in love and moved in together to my place on Wellington I occupied since the beginning of my career. A spacious apartment bathed in light with three bedrooms allowing us ample room to set up a small freelance operation. By now we had purchased another MAC computer. Success is not a fertile delta for self-reflection. I had not hiccupped in my pursuit to land a beautiful position loaded with benefits—until now.

The art director, on 6 month leave, was returning and my job was ending at the Tribune. Sincerely fatigued that hop-scotching into another job was on the horizon, time for some serious thinking. Who was I?

The light bulb went off and I developed a teachable spirit as a result of forfeiting my god-like attitude. Attributing this revelation to the simple fact computers were here to stay and no one cared if I was on the outbound train. But, there had to be more than the box with a motherboard to sustain my drive. Requiring serious self-reflection on how to successfully leverage the sum total of my experiences over the past 10 years, it was by far the hardest truth I faced.

Now it was time to stand up and dance like I meant it—with total conviction. A feeling that would give anyone the heebly-geeblies—pure reality. I easily made transitions to new positions before with the utmost success, but this moment in time felt different. An irrevocable decision with far-reaching repercussions was on the line and I could not clearly define what it was I was deciding. The urge to fast-process and make hasty decisions was dismissed. Before the neurological wiring sends the information to a small pocket of my brain for more extensive evaluation, I created my own version of daydreaming with a crucial need to produce lasting results.

Creative visualization became my gold standard. This exercise needs to legitimately invoke all the senses honestly. And, it needs to surrender fear. What do you want? More importantly, what are you willing to give up?

Knowing that the biological clock was ticking, deductive reasoning told me to head in that direction. You wanted it all, now its time to prove whether you have the guts and stamina. The current speed bump; Keith was freelancing and I was searching and the future relied on certainty. Desiring more permanence and not the cycling in and out of other employer's doors, a relentless ideal of having my own business commingled with the security of a paycheck wrestled around in my head since college. How did this look?

8

Missing Link

Keith was smart, loved to explore the city, and on this fine day was willing to teach me what he had learned about computing art. With my new teachable spirit, and a sincere desire to creatively visualize my life with Mac, Keith and a business, we forged this adventure together. Keith was patient, kind, mathematically in tune, athletic and adored me. In other words, everything I was not and wanted to be. We worked well together—most of the time.

Our nights out included capers of scouring the city with like-minded friends for interesting bars—not "fern bars" referring to yuppie bars popping up all over the northwest side of Chicago. Keith liked to hustle pool, listen to new music and I enjoyed discussions and laughter with anyone who would talk to me for at least 10 minutes at any gin mill of their choosing. A simple time in the city where you could still hear your selections on the jukebox for a quarter and a draft beer was cheap.

Wicker Park happened to be one of our favorite past times. Some joints were still decorated with days of the past—go there today and likely the Rolling Stones had played there when the walls could talk. At least, the bartender might open the drawer revealing some artifact needing no explanation. The Double Door, specifically, was infamous for its ceramic, cheezy Elvis busts along the chair wells of the walls. Gaining entry to the bar was through an ironed-door "buzz-in" system displaying liquor for purchase which led you to a hallway then into the bar. This was not uncommon in the day of gentrification in Wicker Park and Bucktown as old rooming houses were gutted to make way for lofts and yuppie living. The smell had a hidden allure; the contrast of plastic bar stools and housing of tall cracked plaster ceilings, sinks with a drip of water, rats in the alley becomes a memory of dirt and dust in contrast to what the northwest side in the early 90s feverishly changed to in 5 short years. Granite countertops, stainless steel kitchens and new tile in the bathrooms were all the rage, to accent your view of street vermin who pissed on your lawn and sounds of fashionable car alarms.

Chicago invented the contest of who could have the meritorious sounding car alarm. When that contest got old the cars competed for who could have the most insidious base in the trunk. Next contest gave way to who could have the largest flag of their native country waving out the sunroof. Winter in the city and street parking always amused me with the molding selection of furniture or children's toys saving a street-parker's spot they meticulously shoveled for two hours. The unspoken word on the street: remove the piece and we will remove your life. I always had the urge to move someone's place marker just to see what would happen. Still a little too young to take a bullet in the back over an experiment of throwing a plastic bouncy seat from the saved spot to the lawn, the visual fascinated me to an obsession at times.

So, why was all this so glamorous? The suburbs were where the elephants went to die. Having the propensity to want to experience the change and tolerate all the misbehaving one witnessed in lieu of not missing out on all the excitement, the suburbs appeared too far away to be part of the action picturing women making their daily line-up of evening shows to watch on the tube. Maybe a night out included bridge club and talking about diaper rash. Book clubs weren't popular in this genre and I didn't know how to play bridge. I wasn't married yet, so discussing chafing butts was not appealing. People watching and eavesdropping would be terminated from my life. No way. Listening and watching other people was my approach to satisfying a curious nature that allowed me to learn about life.

"City living is where it's at—for now," I gently suggested to Keith. Our friends were buying lofts, townhouses and homes in the city, prompting Keith and I to follow suit. Revealing my lackadaisical nature on certain subjects knowing it prompted a potential conflict, city living was not my final answer.

"I do not want to live in the suburbs," Keith repeated several times in discussions of a conjoined life. Like anyone who doesn't want to hear, I tuned this out believing that he would change his mind once we had children.

Our hidden drive and motive for living in general wasn't to be flashy city slickers, it was to build something unique and sustainable. Grounded in theory based on the past, that meant seeking clients with repeat business. If we were to go the route of building a business, a one-shot logo did not have legs unless it was for a large corporation. Large corporations did not seek "freelancers."

Reminding myself, temperament, environment and personality all play a crucial role in the outcome of success. Keith's steady nature was a leaning post and base for me to diminish the effects of paralyzing fear I could succumb to at times. Keith's soothing demeanor was in direct contrast to my erratic cynical outbursts I found not easy to suppress when the fear level rose steadily. Learning to defer heightened emotions and his ability to censure the outcome, was a critical combination to our initial success. The team was formed with enough opposites to make the union interesting and at this place in time our points of view complemented each other to produce a positive effect.

The proposal. At this moment in time, Keith was offered a job at a design firm in Seattle with a modest paycheck. Whether fear or a deep love for me, he proposed marriage on the rocks at the north end of North Avenue beach. Aww. I said yes. I was employed by the Chicago Tribune as an art director, however rerouting plans to design in Seattle sounded exciting.

The job never happened. Planning a wedding took on a heightened challenge in the face of change. Playing out in my mind was the nagging question, "Did I make the right decision to marry Keith or was it the lesser of two evils?" Not having a husband meant not having children. At 31 years old the selections were dwindling. Our attraction wasn't the endearing type that you hold hands constantly and smooch openly at restaurants. But we did have a mutual respect for our talents, work ethic and desire to have a family. The unique quality as a couple we shared: we could make each other laugh—according to us we were both on genius level. At this stage in our lives we possessed the drive and ambition to make something of our God-given gifts.

Oh, it was quite the affair. A wedding at a Catholic church with all the traditions and a reception at the famed South Shore Cultural Center. Most notably today, Michelle and Barack Obama hosted their wedding reception there exactly eight months after ours—February 29, 1992. The Obama's wedding day was October 3, 1992. The Cultural Center is now a historical landmark and Chicago landmark. The Blues Brother's movie scenes of the Palace Hotel were filmed on the grounds of this beautiful Mediterranean style structure, however my name is probably not on the walls.

A drafty time of change, my intuition proclaimed trust was the fang for securing clients. Once trust took hold, the green light to exercise bold maneuvers and ideas derived from your creative prowess could be unleashed. Not a day before. I also possessed an understanding with myself that perfection was subjective and if I tried to be perfect, the goal of having a business would never be realized. Perfection leads to failure in most studied cases. For that matter, the pure nature of accepting my less-than-flawless existence was at the root of my charm. There is a talent in exposing your vulnerability in a manner that allows you to connect with ax murderers and CEOs, possibly on the same day. I had one skill memorized—known specifically to me as the fine art of listening.

"I have been laid off," Keith said in his usual monotone voice that did not allow me to even remotely guess what the ramifications of this moment had in store. He was by degree and work history an industrial designer.

"What are your plans?' keeping my intense anxiety hidden somewhere between my festering carotid artery and vocal chords.

"Look for a job."

"What type of job? A logical question since the mix of learning the MAC leaned toward graphic design and Keith's tenured, skill set prescribed he was still an industrial designer.

"I'd like to freelance at McDougal Littell, again. I really enjoyed the book publishing we did and I have some experience doing layout." Fair enough wondering where that left the empty MACs sitting in the apartment while the behemoth of technology raced through the industry faster than most could keep up with tirelessly.

Safekeeping the mission to someday have a real business beyond freelancing, cash flow was more important than being a computer expert with no physical work to actually demonstrate output-for-profitability beyond pure speculation. Sitting in the kitchen, looking at the leaf-green walls another roommate of past years painted, the volcano of stress percolated, envisioning another three years in this dumpy apartment. I resided at the same address for eight years now. Not necessarily a horrible notion since moving anywhere in this city was a hassle and an ounce of stability equaled pure gold.

Keith had no shortage of friends and people who genuinely liked him for the same reasons I had fallen in love with him. No question my high-energy personality played symbiotically with his semi somnolent state he appeared to occupy. We all found him soothing and in control—positive that wasn't how they described me. Nonetheless, I became known for my graphic design competence and stature, combined with a new collection of friends with coincidental graphic design titles. Our mutual friend, Jane was a college friend of Keith's from the University of Illinois, party buddy and had grown fond of my charismatic dynamism.

Saved by the bell, again. The bell in 1992 was the phone plugged in to the wall. Remember those? A phone actually rang at a residence.

"Linda we have a freelance opening at First National Bank of Chicago and I have personally suggested you to the head of our department," Jane explained on the phone. The most thrilling point was the effectiveness of networking and having the trust of a friend to make the connection on such a high level. Beats pounding the pavement blindly and opens the door for appearing confident while deep inside I felt like a Zulu warrior.

Located at One North State Street in the heart of the loop, the train stopped right at their door. The marketing department needed qualified help designing corporate collateral pieces creatively, while weaving digital output into each project as technology was driving change at every level of the bank. A warm-bodied soul familiar with presenting to internal clients within a massive banking structure was also helpful—by now it was my claim to fame. A typical project included initiating the copy and overall look of a rack brochure promoting home equities. The complexity of the brochure extended beyond utilizing the brochure for the branches throughout the metro area—its auxiliary pieces could include a statement stuffer, an ad campaign or other ancillary promotional items. In other words, one piece turned into twenty pieces in turn worked out to several clients within the banking structure and a logistical, detail-oriented organizational behemoth. First National Bank of Chicago needed me.

Patting myself on the back, I safely turned on the MAC

without shutting my eyes believing it might begin to smolder. It was an hourly job done on premises with the benefits of constant work and working computers. Keith continued freelancing for the book publisher in Evanston and working out of the house on fictitious computer jobs. Money wasn't as much an issue as learning the Mac and keeping ourselves busy. Rent was still cheap due to the fact I now occupied the same apartment and the landlord enjoyed we paid the rent on time each month without pause.

However, The Great Chicago Flood of 1992 created a severe flood in the loop which included One North State and stopped my gig dead in its tracks. The water flooded into the basements of several Loop office buildings, retail stores and an underground shopping district. The city quickly evacuated the Loop and financial district in fear that electrical wires could short out. Electrical power and natural gas went down or were shut off as a precaution in much of the area. Trading at both the Chicago Board of Trade Building and the Chicago Mercantile Exchange ended in mid-morning, having a global effect, as water seeped into their basements. At its height, some buildings had 40 feet (12 m) of water in their lower levels. However, at the street level there was no water to be seen, as it was all underground.[4]

Basically, I was out of a job. Or was I? The financial industry and visual communicators typically molded together to form a continuous flow of work because all printed material needed updating on a constant basis. Deductive reasoning suggested I hold on to the relationships at the bank and offer to complete the projects underway at home. Keith and I had two computers at our apartment and the bank had virtually shut down corporate communication—at least until the damage was assessed. Seemed like I was in a position to shine. For a couple of months this formula worked until the bank decided the damage was enough to rethink the organization of its corporate communications and I was left with a few projects.

This news left me in a heap. Picking myself up off the ground required severe mental will to push forward and BELIEVE. At this point in time, approximately July of 1992, both of us were virtually clinging to careers. At 32, my tenure as a graphic designer and only a graphic designer, without interruption, paid off.

Saved by the bell, again—one week later.

9

The Stars Align

"Keith, my cousin is the Director of Marketing at a medium-sized bank and is searching for a smaller agency or design firm to execute some of its collateral pieces. Do you have a recommendation?"

"Let me talk to Linda and see what she thinks," said Keith.

Jumping in to action, my visual mind spinning, I knew exactly what this meeting could signify. A defining moment in time knowing the outcome had the dressings of becoming monumental.

The presentation skills and acumen to successfully portray a "yes, we can do that" with a polished spirit and tenured background, was mine to be had. Embracing oddity in the art world no matter what the mundane product may be, doesn't work with the banking set. At least not at the onset of a relationship. Keith was known to reveal his oddities at the wrong time. Not me. A fine arts degree required acting skills and connecting with people—I was an A student with no thespian accolades except the required six credits to graduate. We concluded who the presenter of our meager little freelance operation needed to be.

The incubation stage of a vivid desire to run a design and ad agency was about to give way to reality.

"Hi Lesley, I'm Linda." There was no missing the connection between us, we knew a baby step occurred in the walk toward validating our ability to create something special—in one short moment.

Bright eyes, simple makeup, piercing wit and dressed for success with a crisp blue suit, Lesley embodied the right and left side of the brain working simultaneously—I picked up on this immediately. As a matter of fact, this notion of brilliance made me more determined to walk home with something in my hand.

Time to preach. Making a presentation is like driving a car—you know how to do it, but you best keep your eyes and brain riveted or disaster can occur in an instant. Projects are one-shot endeavors—I was seeking a long term relationship.

"What we are looking for at GreatBank, is to replace our ad agency, which is driving our CEO insane with missing the mark on executing what he envisions," said Lesley. "Not to mention, they are eating our budget with nothing to show for it." My cue was their need. Need is the buzz word. If you can wrap your intentions around the exact purpose for your services and hand in a deliverable that meets expectations, you are golden.

Not recalling the exact moment of triumph or what I said to get there (which is a good thing), I walked out of the initial meeting with a small project. An exponential moment of frisson.

Working within the bank's need of not spending more money than you had to while producing a stunning product, I went to work. Common sense said that if they paid for a brochure, it should have a tangible asset, basically called sales or in the case of banking—new customers. Or in my mind, no tits and glitter or pretty pictures with meaningless words. The bank needs new customers.

"Lesley, let's do a brochure with black and white type that boldly reads, We need You." She laughed that infectious giggle connecting us on another level. Rather, she knew I was real—a deep thinker.

My point of view was to find the least common denominator (the message) and decorate from there. A visual (words or pictures) must stimulate an emotional response in a nanosecond. Humans never fail to remember how they feel—ironically most can't communicate exactly what they feel. Feelings provoke us to move toward something or away from something.

The caveman wasn't a copywriter he was an artist. Visual communication is just that. Words add meaning and assist in the storytelling which is what we have come to expect as evolution dictates.

"The advertising world is going to jump down my throat on this debatable statement—or perhaps cut off my fingers—maybe both." Lesley and I concurred on this statement.

The fang of trust was securely planted in the soul of the bank—they liked me including the CEO, Roger. After all, Roger was cutting the checks. Small projects lead to more projects and within a few short months GreatBank, as we all referred to the banking group, considered completely eliminating their ad agency and rewarding us with more complex problems—GreatBank was motivated to invest in growing its market share in the Chicagoland area and Lesley was the official point person in making that happen. Lesley wrote the copy positioning us for achieving strategic marketing objectives, and I was the creative director supplying the final art for print— strengthening the story. We played role reversal, at times, each writing copy and headlines while envisioning the art. Keith was our computer guru and he could draw. My fiduciary role was assisting in sharpening the arrow to hit the marketing target—with one arrow. After all, that was their basic need. One arrow.

"No layers from an ad agency—just do the work, cut out the nonsense, Linda," said Roger.

"You mean like a farm-to-table approach?" I asked desiring to add a metaphor here and there to showcase my quick wit and intelligence.

"Exactly!"

Hitting walls of resistance is a typical frustration found in ad agencies and any creative or subjective environment dependent upon decisions devoid of emotion. Lesley and I resembled a symbiotic alliance throughout most of our working relationship. Gaining affirmation from the entire banking group added another fang of trust securely in place.

After ten months, it was time to test the corporate

boundaries. A bond we clearly shared together as our relationship and strategies were deemed successful, was a love of travel—and, a love of skiing. We were curious girls, both undergoing an immensely important transition in our careers. Not to mention, boondoggling was fashionable in the early 90's, after all, we worked hard and needed a break. Perhaps, a better analysis of the situation was how do we travel to ski and do a little work? Or, how do we travel and have the company pay for most of the trip?

"Linda, I have to travel to San Francisco the third week of March for a seminar. We're in the middle of redesigning the exterior windows of a few of the branches. I'd like you to design the 'look'. Maybe we can have the company pay for you to go to San Francisco, stay with me at the Fillmore and we'll take photos of banks in the bay area for ideas."

"Let me guess, and then we'll detour over to Tahoe to ski?"

"Yep."

"I'm in."

"You pay for your flight and incorporate the costs into an invoice for our work-in-progress on the signage," Lesley said with an undertone of professionalism disguising a gleeful feeling of we may pull this off and Roger won't hear us spin a yarn of stories.

"Sounds good to me." More work on the horizon, a little bonding with my new best friend and client, and loads of skiing peppered on top.

"Is it necessary to bring all of my photography equipment?" not wanting to botch a detail and appear less-than-competent.

"No, just one lens."

It must have been the grueling winter weather of 1993, that made us laugh and joke while we enjoyed the sunshine of California. The shoot encompassed a few blocks of San Francisco and wrapped in less than twenty minutes. Ultra-efficient in getting work out of the way in order to concentrate on skiing for three full days in Lake Tahoe, I found it necessary to be impassioned enough to be a forever ski partner and keep my favorite client happy. Lesley assumed I was a pro.

My competitive nature and fear of not meeting the expectations of being the great skier I knew Lesley surely was, I put one down.

"Oh yeah, I can do that." A black as the ace of spades run at Squaw Valley with no way out— "no, you can't, Linda," silently gulping to myself harkening back to a pivotal moment at Jackson Hole Mountain two months ago.

A group of friends embarked on a ski trip to Jackson Hole including all levels of expertise at this difficult sport. Distinctly remembering the sobering moment Liz, Paul and I decided to cross check our intermediate skills and ride the tram to the top of the hardest mountain in North America. Duh. The cool factor was all that mattered when we took our place in line to ascend The One, as they say in the ski industry. Stress mounting, sweat building a dam on my thumping heart, the wind picked up and visibility dropped to almost zero as we reached the top.

Liz was an athlete by the purest definition. Paul, being the man, decided he was going to take his chances and go forward with the descent.

"Liz, I'm scared and think I better take the tram down," realizing I was paralyzed with fear and my pride came in second place.

"Me, too." Liz conceded defeat and we both descended the easy route—safely in the tram.

Two months is not enough to get over fear and develop a skier confidence and endurance necessary to ski black runs all day long. Oh well, today was different. Pride was clearly in the lead by a decisive margin.

"Linda, follow me!" Lesley screamed with enthusiasm. Gulp. My new strategy was to ski behind her and mimic her movements. It worked. It worked too well. By 2:30 in the afternoon, the bewitching hour in skier's terms, we were both spent physically. The adrenaline, fist pumping feeling of doing an amazing physical work-out for hours, and I was still upright.

Cruising toward the bottom calling it a day, slush gripped my ski and stopped my forward momentum. Down I went tearing something most certainly. Random hands extended to help me up as I stupidly skied the remaining 300 yards to the lodge. My knee hurt, it swelled within an hour and I knew something was definitely wrong.

"I'm never skiing again!" I said in a veiled demonic tone to Lesley. A three-hour car ride back to San Francisco's airport for our four-hour trip home—in the back of the plane—grimacing in pain, I painfully chose to wait to see a doctor in Chicago. Mainlining Tylenol until I could receive a real X-Ray, the prognosis: a torn MCL and a spirit split like an atom as I exploded in disgust.

A brace for four weeks, and several rounds of physical therapy combined with a grueling schedule allowed for my motivation to track furiously to new heights.

"It's always a good idea to be busy so I don't sit around and ruminate thoughts of self-pity and appear meek," I mentioned to Lesley.

"Great, we have a lot to accomplish."

Aaaaand....we were off to the races. Lesley, Keith and I forged a relationship filled with adventure, learning and working tirelessly to reach new heights with all the tools and resources in place necessary for expanding to a new level.

In 1993 the internet was this busybody lurking out in space and the three of us were drawn to its sexy nature. Not to mention, the illusion of a perfect life loomed large in the minds of opportunists like us—birds of a feather. With many new choices to make, travel and real estate weaved into our minds and stuck like tree sap on your favorite cashmere sweater. It wasn't coming out; throw it away or live with the message. Flashing messages in your mind may never be controlled unless you know someone that has a dry eraser for your brain. The only chance you have to live with messages is to control them, dismiss them, disguise them or reinvent the nagging message into a positive and rename it: curiosity or a thirst for knowledge.

Obvious lifestyle differences are normal when approaching a pivotal time of change. Selecting the most lucrative and positive direction for the immediate future meant the moment of truth was on the horizon for Keith and I.

10

A Fresh Start

The power of a fresh start and desire to own a home/home office was in direct competition to which piece of real estate was priority. Keith's passion for finding a little slice of heaven — a piece of land far, far away from the city, propelled us to travel and look for this elusive place potentially for retirement. Always willing to hide my disappointment until it pops out in malevolent ways, I secretly longed for the traditional suburban home with coffee clubs—oh, the virtue of coffee. However, open to the art of the experience defining my true nature, investing in something beside work for an hourly wage was ultimately attractive setting aside the fantasy of perfection.

Limiting us professionally; a real office as opposed to the apartment meetings which created an illusion of freelance. I desired to promote myself as an agency with the assurance Keith and I could garner the respect necessary to take us seriously as a solid resource. What I didn't want to be was the third party completing other agencies original work.

Our plan for the near future, defined as three weeks or longer, led us to decide we could have both—a home/home office and a slice of land.

Together we had energy—the variety that produces positive results. A tedious search of various neighborhoods on the north side of Chicago including a variety of dilapidated structures, we found a two-flat in Old Irving Park on a commercial street allowing us to have an office on the first floor. The second floor was livable to the point we could occupy it while we renovated to a higher standard of living than moldy carpet and a pre-war kitchen. Included in the deal with any 90-year old building was cloth wiring, asbestos siding and special antiques and challenges not suitable for the faint-of-heart.

Acting instinctively and swiftly in a decision to purchase this property, the first floor had beautiful hardwood floors and a presentable space for the office. No special design in mind, it communicated stability and a workable floor plan for growth.

"If you are going to put in a dishwasher and two computers and any other devices, you will need to open these walls and replace with Romex®," said the contractor we consulted for Plan A. He was smiling with a slight smirk—not always a good sign.

"Ugh—do we need this massive upgrade right now?" Thinking to myself, why did we think this whole renovating thing was a good idea? Oh yeah— forward progress inching our way toward a modest feeling of security.

We had so little money to scrape together. The two-flat was $106,000. and the cheapest piece of livable real estate in an up-and-coming neighborhood on the north side of Chicago. The banks allowed a 5% down payment in 1993. With $6,000 to our name, realistically we had $500 left over for renovations and a few outstanding invoices—oops! The hell of renovation began and the creative financing to cover the $5,000 electrical upgrade is a fuzzy memory. We borrowed from everyone with a smile, handshake and lovable gesture assuring them they would get paid back.

Feeling like I was taking the current out to sea no matter where it leads, we slept in the attic while they tore apart the plaster walls for new electric. The attic was crude at best, but it worked for sleeping quarters even though we woke up each morning chewing on plaster dust wondering what the nutritional value of eating 90-year-old plaster yielded and its inherent risk. The whole scene was an act of perseverance, better known as calculated risk.

Self-respect was at stake since we didn't have a whole lot of support from family for even buying a "roach" with the magnitude of its undertaking to make it livable. My brother, Michael, suggested we take a match, sweep it up and start over. Too bad it wasn't legal.

And, then a miracle occurred. After months of electrical

nightmares and a semi-functioning kitchen, we attempted to refinance. Six months had passed—the required time before you were allowed to refinance an existing loan in the banking environment of 1994.

Of course, my largest client was Lesley and GreatBank. Whether they should or could, they refinanced our loan. The math was simple. $106,000. purchase price minus our 5300. down payment brought the original loan at purchase to 100,600. The appraised value of our renovations and upgrades made the new value $137,000. Phew! The new $127,000. meant we had $10,000. in cash to walk out the door of our second closing and a boost of real estate confidence.

Several people had their hand out before we started the car or bellied up to the nearest bar. The triumphant feeling of success paying debtors the small amount we owed went a long way in reinforcing this new-found confidence. The paltry $5,000 left over after debt, went directly to further renovations. Precariously selecting which room needed the most attention, the kitchen was redesigned with the help of my cousin Mary Kay who owned a high-end distributorship of appliances. Luck prevailed. What potentially could have cost $10,000. became $5,000. Not to mention, our designer eyes created a first-rate look for the least amount of outlay in cash. Knocking out walls ourselves and rebuilding pieces to garner a loft-feeling, screaming hip even though the metal cabinets of yesteryear and plumbing jimmy-rigged for a dishwasher were still in place.

We had a long way to go—the exterior reeked of inner city ghetto. Ahh, the vigor of youth and a "just do it" attitude.

Back in the day, taxes in Chicago were nationally less expensive than our west coast and east coast neighbors. You didn't get much for your tax dollars—garbage pick-up was the one thing you could count on—everything else was on your own dime, like proper schooling for your kids. The decision to live in the city for work was the final answer and I was prepared to adhere to this adjudication and move forward with all its glories and sullen absurdities.

The pressure valve was released, the business flowed in and the taxes and mortgage were easily achieved. We began pitching for larger projects which meant more detailed briefs and discovered Keith could easily fulfill the computer work necessary to present the assumption we were officially established. The key factor of our success was that we were producing results.

The power of systems and organization were beginning to pay off, always insistent that consistency is one of the keys to success. For that matter, a firm hand never wavering under the conditions of the moment, it sends a clear message to employees and clients that trust is realistically the epitome of truth if you want to reveal what is actually attached to the bottom line.

A project management log worth its weight in gold, I learned an effective system of keeping track of projects, budgets and billings from a successful design firm still in existence today. VSA was built on discipline and consistency. Having the fortunate experience working within VSA's system, I adopted the matrix which became the backbone of keeping multiple projects on time and budget not to mention a sense of sanity in the ever-changing world of advertising and design. Slop would not cross the threshold of this office. Nor would anything less than stellar work leave the premises.

Lurking out there was how Keith and I would combine our clients to form a corporation and structure the business. Agreeing with our CPA that forming a corporation was the sensible approach to handling the income, I insisted this could only occur with a detailed business plan. My theory: no business plan, plan to fail. We had come too far at this point to regress.

"We don't need a business plan!" Keith insisted.

"I believe it's the only way to exist and evaluate our

forward progress. It's like a detailed map with your mission and goals attached. When you get lost it's easy to examine where the wrong turn occurred. Not to mention, if we expect to get a line of credit for any expansion or new equipment, the bank will require a detailed plan."

Keith resisted plans. I loved them. The first sign of strife and opposing opinions left me with no option but to sit down and hash out a plan alone—25 pages to be exact. My demand for moving forward in unison. Included in the plan was a sophisticated spread sheet. Detailed accounting numbers are not my expertise, therefore Keith took this responsibility and task to an A+ polished level. Every bookkeeping number was exact and "footed." In fact, it was always clear and concise and we knew where we stood financially from every angle on any given day. The computer was slowly becoming my friend realizing its multi-faceted value and the power of Excel. I didn't want to be the cockle in the fabric, computers were becoming our employees and Keith's obsessive attention to detail was an asset to the business.

Lesley was impressed with the business plan solidifying our position of appearing stable and fastidious. Order will always trump chaos.

Keith was bringing in business from Motorola, Anixter— all companies with high-profile projects—he had the inside track to "friends in high places." Rewards for toiling, sophisticated time management skills and a dedication to critical thinking over the smallest decisions were now clearly visible at the bottom line. Again, results spoke the loudest and rewarded us with top-tier clients and the ability to progress at a steady pace.

In direct contrast to all this discipline, the right side of my brain began to sizzle with an itch motioning I was having unattended moments in the travel world. Basically, I wanted to hitch a ride to some Bohemian tribal Community.

Or, should I opt for an atoll in the South Pacific complete with awakening to a fleet of servants—most importantly the Executive Chef reciting an exotic dish prepared especially for my now-developed, sophisticated palate.

"I hate when these fantasies happen," beating myself. "Well, let's turn it into a positive with critical thinking," noticing I was beginning to talk to myself—hand gestures and mouth movements included.

Repositioning consciousness is not always a bad thing, it reminds us that we have two sides to our soul. The first side demands order, the second side seeks the unknown clinging to the safety of order. It's not a mental health issue, it's how we form the perfect circle of life and protect ourselves. Some people can exit with the sameness each day—I could not. Neither could Keith. Another feature of our connectedness as a couple.

"Now that the business is in order, and our subcontractors can handle our absence, do you think we should go back to Driggs and look at a few pieces of property?"

Together, we concurred, combining wanderlust and real estate offices in the United States, Idaho was the clear winner in seeking a slice of land for our future. It was 1994 and Driggs the county seat in Teton County the locals call Teton Valley, forty five minutes from Jackson, Wyoming had the quintessential pattern of future growth gleaning from our due diligence and my tireless effort of absorbing and storing information with the help of a photographic memory.

The internet would certainly play a factor in expansion beyond Jackson Hole as it appeared the changing world would allow for remote work. We assumed the cubicle would disintegrate. Jackson was expensive and the drive over the hair-raising pass made Driggs the logical choice for purchasing property. A goal we were going to make happen, not to mention a reward for adhering to discipline and clearing hurdles larger than behemoths. It's important to give success as much weight as we do all the finite problems solved day in day out.

Travel has a mood-lifting effect. And, reaching the waning days of sunlight after summer solstice always precipitates a need to make plans for the tortuous winter ahead in Chicago. Time to plan a ski trip and review the few pieces of land the realtor sent in the mail—no internet in the 90's. Nope, did things the old-fashioned way—mail and thermal paper faxes—a fabulous form of entertainment we say, "meh" to today. The delay of information would make a teenager today refer to it as the horse and buggy era. We lunged for the newspaper and mailbox each morning. Imagine that.

The Grand Teton mountain range loomed large over Teton Valley, Idaho. A vacant and harsh feeling palled over the valley floor—perfect for exploring, not for explaining why we chose this place. If the clouds erased the four peaks and a fog settled thin over the valley bottom it looked like a scene from Little House on the Prairie. At this time, there were only a few two story houses built. Farmers were succumbing to selling out to developer's subdivisions more lucrative than potatoes.

We could always amend the plan and purchase in another area of the country if things went awry. Specifically, why we chose to spend $20,0000 on our purchase of raw land and not break the bank we precariously owned.

Distinctly remembering how we unconventionally achieved a small pittance of savings; we arranged to have $250. sent monthly to a remote savings account from our checking account at the corner bank. No ATM card attached, we amassed a mere $2,000. in a short time by adding to the account and never withdrawing a penny.

Our decisions were a sincere effort to keep focused on our future and finalize any piece of land with a keen eye on the business and family that surely would follow soon. Still living the on-going debate crawling underneath my thin skin: can I have it all or is it just an illusion?

Telling myself, "this motivation has to segway in to nomenclature that suggests arranging the people I trust to get things done in the desired time frame with a limited budget."

The three skills attached to my soul were love, integrity and logic. Time to put them to good use.

Keith worked hard and toiled until he hit perfection. I, on the other hand, had the attention span of a flea with an obstructive bowel. I learned to live with this deficit and produce positive results. Ideas were never a shortcoming—I could think and visualize the outcome. People stating the obvious was an irritant and an insult to my intelligence.

"I have an idea, Keith," hoping for his favorable listening skills to appear. " I think Michael would love to come with us to Idaho."

Michael is my brother. The brother you share experiences, laugh and cohort to the fullest that life has to offer. Water-skiing, snow-skiing, traveling, sailing and our love of food—good food. We'd venture into rotten, forbidden areas of the city for "the real deal" as we referred to a tasty treat.

His claim to fame with Keith and I; he was a master carpenter. We would've loved to employ him for our first project on Pulaski, however, he currently enjoyed a lucrative job on the North Shore of Chicago building high-end homes. Michaels' baffled looks and sullen comments always provided a subtle source of laughter.

"That place is a roach. Call me when you have a real house," learning to deal with his outbursts knowing he never really meant what he said.

Michael was a buffoon in a pink tutu. Never mollycoddled, I knew underneath all the gruff was a sensitive soul and a willing partner in helping his only sister succeed, regardless of her real estate shortcomings to date.

Time for my highly persuasive personality to show up—I

discerned from other shoddy contractors, Keith, Michael and I could build great things together. I valued his opinion and he eventually softened up to meet me halfway on most issues we bantered. Wickedly sarcastic, his intimidation factor lasted for a nanosecond—and vice versa. We had this bond.

Success rarely goes from point A to point B—it's a crooked road and Michael and I discussed this theory at length. "If it was easy, everyone would be doing the same thing," his famous words. Agreed. Seeking to entice him into constructing a new bathroom we desperately needed on the second floor of the "roach" we called home, I needed time to remind him of his major league craftsmanship.

"Michael will you come with us to Driggs to look at land? We'll pay for your trip and you'll see how awesome the snowboarding at Grand Targhee and its famous powder is all about. Pleasssseee?"

"I'm not building anything out there. Period!"

"I know, consider it an adventure," my true advertising prowess showing up to persuade him and note the emotional benefits. He was as curious as I was and I knew this to be true. I inherited a collection of family and friends that shared this intimate desire to be out there.

"Rule number one: no camera. You know I won't have patience to stop anywhere while we wait for you to shoot," he said smugly.

"Promise. Whaaaa!!" We had a deal.

Travel always involved schlepping my camera equipment—most people hated all my props. At times relaxing and observing the scene stored images for shots in the future. I left the camera at home, as promised, frenzied that I may have missed a good one and a moment in time was stolen forever. Shooting photos was not some new frivolity for me—Michael knew it was a passion and had been for years.

11

More Than This

My dear friend Nancy from grade school, was always the willing and able partner for exotic reaches of the United States and beyond our borders—she was the ultimate partner in patience and catered to my insatiable desire to bring along my photo equipment.

Nancy had no desire to have kids and had a lucrative nursing job that allowed ample time off; our claim to fame—people would stop and ask if we were twins. This wasn't our only match—we loved to hop in the car and do a road trip.

At 16 years old we shared the same joy and vitality for life with a crackled laugh. Small things humored us, and the big city was down the Kennedy Expressway—a paycheck away from IMagnum at Michigan and Oak—where the beautiful and well-heeled in Chicago shopped. Truth be told, I felt sorry for her when they said we looked alike—she was stunningly beautiful; high cheek bones and a chiseled nose, voluptuous body and perfect features—most times I felt like a frump next to her. Nancy loved the finer things especially when it came to makeup and clothes—spare no expense. We were making great money at 16 years old compared to our contemporaries.

We shared the curiosity of how others lived. Luck or being in the right place at the right time seemed to perpetuate this passion—by now I had a track record. Her vision of travel intersected mine at the exact point necessary for a seamless experience. We never made hotel reservations—how could we do that when we didn't know where we would be on any given night?

Luck was on our side in 1987, at 27 years old and this fine spring night at the Merchandise Mart in Chicago.

In the magazine business you always received invites to various functions. Tonight, I imbibed on a pass to the Apparel Mart's 10th anniversary party held at the Merchandise Mart. Arriving late, the admission for entry included holding on to a raffle stub for giveaways at the end of the night. To this day I believe that the lateness of my raffle ticket made it sit on top of the batch ready to be drawn first.

The Grand Prize: 2 round-trip tickets on American Airlines to anywhere in Europe. My name was drawn as the grand prize winner and Nancy was the chosen partner for the two-week adventure. Why? Simply because she knew it would involve bringing my camera equipment and taking pictures of "things" most would not be patient enough to endure while I strategically set up the shot. These scenes occurred every day in Italy and Switzerland.

"Pull over." I screamed

"Oh my God, why?" she laughed.

"You know...I see something."

"OK, take your photo. I don't see anything, but I know you must see something invisible." Nancy always pulled over.

This foray into photography pivotally made an impact on the rest of my career. God bless Nancy today for being patient—she understood my insatiable desire to perform. I trusted her understanding that a few shots do seem like vaporous objects are going to descend from the sky and make themselves present. Instinct is one of the secret ingredients to a powerful photo.

Lighting and its instantaneous moment of creating a mood combines this instinct with the snap of the shutter. Landscape photography and my patented formula of anticipating these moments launched a subset of my design career. By this time, in the late 80's I had accumulated over 2,000 slides. Subsequently over the next ten years several of the shots appeared in national magazines, collateral pieces for distinguished client's in our design firm, a show downtown and large images on family and friend's walls.

Potentially, reason number 2 had surfaced as to why Driggs and Jackson, Wyoming in 1994 became the ultimate choice in a land acquisition. Lighting was everything to my photo success, and this place had it going on like nowhere else in the lower 48 states. An artist's paradise, you could locate tripod holes in the ground where some of the famous mountain scenes of the Tetons were recently shot by photographers. I enjoyed myself looking for these tripod stamps empowering my belief the easy road is right in front of us—the hard road includes enlarging your perspective.

Swallowed up by its dynamic features, the landscape and wide open spaces became the ultimate allure of curiosity. Keith concurred this place, Driggs is magical and virtually only 5% of the population has ever heard it exists. He was more the mountaineer and I was simply a wannabe viewing the purchase of land and its symbol of freedom in direct contrast to the crowded city, sirens blaring, screams from the unknown and my all-time favorite symbol of chaos: the helicopter. Typically, the helicopter in Chicago was a badge of disappointment feigning little fissures in my soul.

Standing on the edge of a monumental change, we were about to purchase a second piece of property. Adhering to my own mantra, silencing the exterior forces of evil known as negative messages, I once again understood perspective is enlarged through tedious, hard work combined with fabulous deductive reasoning skills. All innate personality traits are God-given, developing what you don't have overcomes challenges producing results.

Precisely why I love to read, consume information through experience and learn through the school of hard knocks which message is compensable and which one clearly should be discarded. This lesson for mankind is lifelong, better defined as our own struggle dujour. Never believe the next guy doesn't struggle—that IS an illusion.

At hand was the motivating theory I searched to prove. Can I have it all? The visual needed clarity and the subconscious mind, feelings of satisfaction and execution were steadily coming into focus. The true paradigm of change has yet to be realized. Currently, I was doing the exercises and homework before the big test.

"Michael, I'm pregnant.... the baby is due in April. Please help us put in a bathroom."

"How are you going skiing in January if you're pregnant?" He chided me with a profound question expecting a rational answer.

"We've done our homework, have a little money saved and the two-flat has gained appreciation by approximately 5% since we refinanced."

Believing in the accuracy of our astute research in the neighborhood, a business that was steadily gaining credibility, and a focus on spending fastidiously while investing every penny wisely, we committed to moving forward.

"Michael will you please renovate our bathroom before the baby comes? The bathroom is full of lead paint and needs to be gutted."

"You're crazy. Ok, here are my rules. I give you a list and when I ask for something you're there to get it from the lumberyard, paint store, electrical—anything I need. Second rule, stay out of my way. Third rule, you do all the clean-up."

"That's it?" I exclaimed with a smile stretched ear to ear.

"Oh yeah, you pay me on time every time. No begging."

"Deal." I honored this relationship would work, and if it didn't it was just a bathroom—we had enormous amounts of renovation to bring the place to where I'd even allow a client to have a meeting in our conference room.

For all the hassles we were guaranteed a superior bathroom with the "king"—his self-described nickname. Knowing how much Michael adored me, he threw in extras to solidify our unspoken bond. Always.

"Are you going to Driggs with us in January, Mikey?"

"Wouldn't miss it. Sign me up."

The bathroom began in September of 1994 and was completed two months later. Beautiful, simple, on budget and spoke volumes of an unwavering extension of trust and its rewards—progress.

Thanksgiving 1994—I displayed the tiniest indication of a pregnant woman and hormonal strength to accomplish the unimaginable. Diligently working·· 8·10 hours a day, making plans to complete the task of travel to the wilderness, land was the symbol of putting a down payment on our future. Pushing the limits of human brain input typically an indication my head would pop off, I reacted to a new brain sizzle; acquire my real estate license. The goal wasn't to sell real estate, but to learn and absorb information. Basically the only thing put on the back burner was how to solve world hunger. Next year.

Hormones and adrenaline are a magic elixir producing super·human traits, and on most occasions I uniquely fit through the opening to this universe only a few would enter. The "crazy creative" was not the label I loved—it's what I lived with knowing my common sense skills kept me tethered to the planet and ensured goodwill for anyone who followed along with my ideas.

January, February and March of 1995 proved a colossal of dreams, ideas and goals necessary to clearly wrap myself around the impending birth of my first child in April.

Perfection is only a perception from my point of view. Time management, keeping the balls in the air and focusing intently on what is right in front of you allows for magic to occur.

"Focus goes a long way in making short order of a task," says the girl with self·diagnosed ADD. Practicing focus relied heavily on my list of priorities similar to the 4 points I utilized in the past to graduate from college.

Some people viewed my outward persona as someone who didn't know enough to come in out of the rain—flighty was an adjective and undertone. Too bad. I knew differently, felt differently and acted differently, somehow dismissing the criticism cruelly launched. The deep root was firmly planted, the tree was showing signs of life and the rewards of having it all were a short distance away from being fully tested.

To date my job description was rather ragged and somewhat incongruent. Business-owner, pregnant carpenter, real estate entrepreneur, creative director, and soon-to-be: mommy. And, the nagging personality disorder I firmly possess was itching at me developing a rash on my heart: competing. It was 12 weeks before my due date.

At this point, I had been to 48 states and Keith had been to 47. Not an intense goal on the forefront of priorities, however, breathing down my neck in a manner not dismissible was our dear friend Norm Bob. Norm loved to travel with passion and purpose, and so did his lovely wife, Linda.

They were our best friends and by now we had collected several states together. We were all in our 30's, making great salaries, and most of us did not have children, the perfect recipe for seeking unique travel destinations typical Americans could care less about. Or, pinpointing states, rounding out our collective goal of seeing all 50 states. I hated to lose this contest to Norm. A gentlemen's trophy was bragging rights.

Norm and Linda were the inspiring personalities who clearly made the list of people you wanted to spend time on vacation with—Norm was in charge of the to-do list. Each activity had the complexity to the point it should have been designated its own day. Nope. You needed stamina and perseverance because that meant 25 notable activities occurred on a trip of five days. In reflection, the value in memories vividly present today, we could never discredit his amazing prowess to satisfy the crowd.

He was also a photographer and an engineer, therefore providing tremendous inspiration and motivation. Funniest people on the planet—we could make each other laugh until the wee hours of the morning.

Norm and I loved to compete. We manufactured fun. On

a recent trip to Vermont, biking to see the colors of fall, he forced me to stay up all night playing Big Boggles. I was in first place and he was in second—torture for him. I humored Norm into thinking he could beat me. False. We called it quits at 3 a.m. Now, being a fierce competitor with Norm, I was not going to let him win the state contest. We made stringent rules with an unspoken handshake, not to break them. Landing at an airport to make a connection did not count as a state. Never; a meal in that state is required in order for a new state to count. Of course, we didn't have any way of cross-checking your newest acquisition—winners need not apply if you are prone to cheating. If you saw the state when you were three and could not recall anything about that place—our rule: go back to the state. No cheating.

Our traveling buddies were storytellers enjoying the laughter and inquisitive nature of each other. The why and the how made the difference in whether we listened or replied, "meh." It was that simple and yet so powerful. My baby was due in 12 weeks.

Keith and I had a trip planned to Boston in October of 1995, Maine would be my 49th state and sure to be on the agenda this fall.

My 50th state would be North Dakota. The cogs of my brain combined with extra-duty hormones concocted a plan. With Mileage Plus®, I had enough miles to travel to Fargo, North Dakota—after all it only needed to be a meal according to the rules. On February 9, 1995, I flew to Fargo for the night. Negative 9 degrees outside, 7 months pregnant staying at the downtown Holiday Inn, the casino downstairs was an obvious selection. Not much of a gambler beside some of the risks of life, I won enough to have a luxurious breakfast with room service before my flight back to Chicago, knowing the trophy of gloating was yet to come.

12

··

Dismissing Perfection

From the day Amelia was born (well 3 days after 6:44 pm on April 27, 1995) I was a full time mom, full time entrepreneur on a 24-hour clock living the best of both worlds. Proving my theory that potentially you can have it all—still a sophomore with lessons unknown and snags of chaos to be conquered. The visual of sitting at my computer on April 30th with Amelia tightly wrapped in a snuggly on my chest is indelible. However productive the work output, it enflamed an aha moment with an enjoyment in the search for meaning— having it all was culminating with good fortune. The reality clearly depended on a cocktail each morning of the strongest coffee on the market improving the odds of making it through the day without a nap.

If she became fussy I'd make up the work at 5 a.m. or after she went to bed, experiencing complete flexibility— step one. This arrangement allowed being present in the moment—the highest challenge was the constant juggling act, with the pay off becoming clearer. The true joy of living in the city—no commuting except under my conditions—not during rush hour. So far so good on the having-it-all theory.

The shift of priority lay in my arms. One of the most powerful and magical transpirations of bringing new life into the world is the deep sense of responsibility transforming our soul into a call-to-action chariot. Parents are consistently summoned to keep their kid's safe no matter what—no small task. There is no retraction clause to parenthood. Final decisions would coalesce Amelia and her future for the next eighteen years.

At hand was an infant, a growing business with incorporation papers ready to sign, combined with a final decision on which piece of property we would purchase in Driggs. Adrenaline flow seasoned my mind with a virtue and talent I will forever be grateful—extreme focus.

Amelia, now three months old was a sleeper and so was I,

therefore, sleep deprivation was not a contender in throwing off my rituals and staying on task—ADD seemed to disappear and rising to new heights inspired me to succeed.

The expectations put on myself and Keith found us waddling through what we just created, trusting we were right. Life-changing decisions and documents circled the conference table, with the foundation firmly cemented, all were awaiting our signatures. These are the exact moments of trust and believing in yourself no matter how paralyzing the pressure engulfs you and brings you to your knees.

"Sign here," motioning to Keith, referring to the closing papers on our 1.0 acre property. Simultaneously we each signed. The following day we signed the papers and became Gebhardt Kraus & Associates, Inc.

A few hurdles complete, a seismic shift could be felt in our sense of purpose elevating us to the highest point ever experienced—a new baby has that effect. Like juggling, the moment you take your eye off one ball the show is officially over. The shift in behavior mandated consistency leaning toward practicality with each decision. And each decision required teamwork, compromise and accountability.

"Successful musicians always seem to be able to get away with flirting with new art forms and find themselves remaining relevant," I pontificated with Lesley as we discussed the new business now known as GKA, Inc. Searching for something unknown that clogged the bands of my right and left brain, Lesley was known to bring me back to the center. Lesley was my biggest fan, reminding me that each brick was meticulously laid to form the foundation we created. "Now, may be the time to expand our potential—but how?"

"Here is where a business plan becomes the ultimate tool of success," I stated pondering my own statement. Then, in true form my mind wandered to places only philosophers dare untangle.

"We don't want to lose the imaginative sensory each of us possess," I concluded with an antipodal strategy, knowing these concepts are opposites but belong to the same circle. "After all we were creatives first and business people second, and these two typically don't match."

"Stay focused and remind yourself how you got to this level in the first place," she said with a confirmed reaction to my space odyssey. "The bank loves you and all you have accomplished with us in the past three years."

"Trust is visceral, Lesley." I gently needed to remind myself the finer points of exactly how I did get to this plateau deserved reverence, however reaching new levels itched at my brain. Practicality was one necessary ingredient to run the marathon, but the what-ifs out there created an internal tension between me, myself and I. Sometimes to the point of feeling like the scrape of old metal on a gaping open wound. The challenge was circumventing these notions into a leadership position for the benefit of the team. "Moments of ecstasy" were elusive goals and I knew when the arrived.

Keeping the bullet points fresh, moving forward each day, new personal goals needed to seamlessly mesh with business and family interests. This meant the picture better make sense or nothing is going to get accomplished. A business must always be in a pattern of growth or it loses its relevancy.

Lesley's face told the story more passionately than her statement, "We need to put you in front of the other president's group-wide. I may not be with the bank much longer." You need to whimper a little cry of pleasure when the siren of opportunity blares.

"I have an MBA from one of the top schools in the country and basically there are banks out there that want to consider my worth."

"I'm screwed," I said to myself knowing what the ramifications of this meant. Potentially losing a client. She was my point person. She was the main source of cash flow on a monthly basis. Not wanting to walk straight into the jaws of failure, tension and fear riddling my sense of security, I knew the comfort of the past three years hit major turbulence.

"Linda, you have to reach out in the organization and develop relationships with the other banking units. I'll start facilitating meetings and introducing you to the presidents of the other banks. You also should consider expanding into other areas of expertise. You can't rely on my being your only client—it won't work."

The first sign of change was on the horizon. "She's right, we can't think everything is going to stay the same. Duh." I loved to talk to myself, prompting an actionable plan with a dismount the judges would surely give a solid ten, not wanting to spend the next several years fixing a critical mistake we could have circumvented at the very intersection of opportunity.

Interruptions are a fact of llfe, learning to sort out what has priority at any given second is a skill, once mastered installs trust for anyone who admires accomplishments desiring to be part of your plan—better described as leadership qualities.

Deductive reasoning extrapolated from the past success said it was time to write out at least three main messages and potentially scribble them on the wall in indelible marker—maybe invent new wallpaper. Creative visualization can become fuzzy unless these messages are clear and dominate the visual. Similar to a coach in any sport who is motivated to win and believes a message is the differentiating ingredient; his message in crucial moments of win or lose, ignites the strongest-willed engines to accelerate above the situation—best illustrated in a one-point basketball game with 4.5 seconds left.

13

Fear is the Enemy of Progress

S eeking to have good fortune and a pleasant environment engaging work and parenthood, I forged a new mantra, discarding fear as the enemy of progress. Herein lies my talent and virtues once again showing up to the party: focus and storing memories in my mind. Utilizing bullet points as the secondary option, I chose to render a rough visual of the overall picture to date.

On August 4, 1995 my birthday gift to myself was the creation of this very visual providing a glimpse and detailed inventory of our accomplishments to date similar to retail executives doing inventory after a chaotic Christmas season. At 35 years old here's what it looked like: no assistant, performing this exercise all by myself. I craved certainty amongst the chaos—knowing it wasn't remotely realistic— just a reward.

Positioning myself for the beginning of my self-appointed tour out on the bustling sidewalk that met the curb of the two-flat on Pulaski Road in Chicago—three feet in back of me traffic swept by and the full-flavored smell of bus fumes lingered in the air.

"Funny we rarely spent any time out here except to get the mail, check on some noisy nonsense occurring at the bar three doors down or review weedy landscaping that was in much need of attention and possessed no urgency on our to-do list," talking to myself. I pretended there was someone standing beside me taking notes. My mind worked like a retention pond capable of retaining hoards of visual information. I was invested in the notion my photographic memory would never go dry.

Directly behind me across the street was Section 8 housing, mostly Middle Easterners who parked their cabs on Pulaski. They dressed in American-looking clothes, saris and some in full burqua. Peaceful people, typically only surfacing on Friday as the men walked two blocks to the mosque for prayers. The dusty mauve, four-story building was relatively well-kept except for the occasional graffiti the landlord ritually painted over. The location served their cab-driver profession. We were three blocks from the entrance to the Kennedy Expressway and ten minutes to the terminals at O'Hare Airport on a day without traffic. We never spoke to each other except maybe a nod and a wave—we couldn't. The food they purchased was from a store next to the mosque selling saris and various sundries. I curiously wandered into the store when we first moved to the neighborhood overwhelmed with its disheveled appearance and food items in a foreign language. The smell would have knocked you out.

Amusing myself with this sensory overload, standing in the same position on the sidewalk, pivoting I looked to the right of our building. Next door was a brick, three-story 5-unit apartment building owned by the Patels who lived in the first floor unit with a kitchen window that faced our backyard. The distance between that window and our chain-linked fence was exactly five feet. The front of the building on the first floor was their laundry mat and viable source of income in addition to renters. Our cozy existence never really bothered me because Mrs. Patel and her two teenage children loved us and ogled over Amelia. I amused myself watching Mr. Patel mow his 20 ft. by 20 ft. lawn with one arm—never truly understanding what happened to his lame arm because communication between us was stifled by language barriers.

Chuckling to myself, while executing this visual exercise, hearing my mom's reaction to watching Mr. Patel mow his lawn if she came by and sat in our backyard. "He's down an arm. Why don't his kids do that job?"

"I don't know," laughing at her cynicism, "maybe it's their culture."

There is a certain acceptance of urban living you either love or hate. In our neighborhood of choice, the front of the house and all its urban nonsense did not match the streets directly in back of the house. Well kept residential avenues with kids playing outside, manicured lawns and porches filled with folks waving even if they didn't know your name.

I often chuckled to people when they asked about our decision to purchase here, "it's not like the ice cream truck plays 'Helter Skelter'."

Keith took up issue with Mr. Patel because he made money from the wall murals of advertising on the brick facing of his building we stared at from our office window. Two 20 ft. horizontal ads were changed periodically and the people who put them up and took them down—a messy job—had to prop their ladder on our property to manage without killing themselves. Keith had a point, but a point of contention? Curious.

Ah, and the grand dame of the neighborhood and source of everlasting humor, the house to the left of where I was standing—Bob's house. This wasn't really Bob's house, but his elderly and ill sister's house. Bob resided here 90% of the time in order to hide his drinking habit from his wife who lived two miles away in Wicker Park. Bob claimed that his sister's children never visited mom or took care of anything. From my perspective neither did he, except for the annuals planted every spring like symbols of toiling hoping no one really noticed there were a total of 6 plants. Most of the plants he brought home from work were left on my porch— greatly appreciating this gesture.

Bob's posture was slightly tilted 15 degrees toward the ground, his forefinger routinely adjusted his glasses so they wouldn't fall off his nose and he talked at you with a slur. Never did catch his age but his deep wrinkles from a weathered face working outside in "Grandmas Garden" at the Lincoln Park Conservatory suggested perhaps 60ish. He was categorically a piece of work. We loved his kind nature, and amusing antics. Always a source of entertainment he made us all roar with laughter reminding me of a particularly funny scene.

"Linda your lawn mower is broken, it won't cut my grass," he slurred while returning our electric mower.

"Bob, it works better when its plugged in," laughing—Keith and I watched from the second floor as he tried to mow the lawn without plugging it in—the cord wiggling and trailing behind the mower.

"Oh, I thought I did that." It was hard to keep a straight face. Note: never attempt to cut the lawn buzzed unless you want to do it twice.

Bob's house was surviving its functional life—barely. Built in 1908 in the classic farmhouse style to house a burgeoning family, few improvements were obvious on the exterior, aside from the necessities like siding and windows. What the inside looked like was up to anyone who dare use their imagination. Bob smoked heavily in the home and it appeared the strategy was to let the house decay naturally because Lucille, his sister would pass soon.

The siding was the same asbestos asphalt our two-flat acquired as an alternative to replacing the beautiful original lap wood. Removing it would require a hazmat team. "That can't be cheap," I muttered. The beautiful shade of moss green popular in the 30s, looked like some animal had been gnawing on its ridges originally designed to look like fake wood, now the grime of the city made it appear like blackened green tar.

Our siding was no different. First thought upon entering to take inventory of all the unequivocal good points our place had done for us, "what are we going to do with four floors of this special asphalt siding?" Positive the warranty had expired—a lifetime warranty in the 30s meant 30 years, not 70. The architects did not factor these buildings would last 100 years. Attempt to power wash knowing it was a subtle fix? This is not sufficient in making a difference in the curb appeal.

A sick feeling of "so much needs to be done," began to

overwhelm me even before I walked in the front entrance. The dance between a heavy overwhelmed feeling and a sense of pride in all our accomplishments to date nearly crushed me. "Never," reminding myself why this current exercise was so necessary for my psyche—my birthday present.

The ultimate decision to purchase on a busy street; the commercial zoning dictated by the city of Chicago stating a viable business cannot have daily, in/out traffic (FedEx, UPS) on a residential street and remain a business without proper licensing. By now we had freelancers, clients and daily deliveries. Someone on a residential street would have blown the whistle and put us out of business immediately until we found the appropriate commercial space for our enterprise. "That's right," talking to myself qualifying this decision and the high price tag of harder-than-average toiling while enjoying the sweet smell of bus fumes.

Standing on the porch expanding the entire front of the house, one huge improvement was a forest green, all glass storm door exposing a beautiful original two-inch thick, antique oak wood door. From the street view, it offered very little in the way of transforming the appearance of ghetto if you were quickly driving by, but the newness spoke hip and modern. And, my favorite tidbit of renovation: two brand new, white, shiny identical mailboxes purchased from Restoration Hardware—placed side by side; one for GKA and one for us personally. Small, new things pleasured me, giving meaning to the book I read recently, *The Tipping Point*, by Malcolm Gladwell.[2] Specifically states the theory behind New York City revitalizing their ghettos, reducing horrendous crime, begins with the small things making the biggest difference. Theorizing, repairing broken windows signifies change in a positive direction as opposed to continued decay. The shiny new mailboxes symbolized change like a badge.

The vestibule, an extremely small space in most two and three flats of the era, beyond the front door, held two more doors. The second door lead to the stairs ascending to our second floor apartment and our pink living room.

The first floor had its own entrance and opened to our famous conference room. Famous for the many people who now crossed the threshold of our glorious business. Crisp white trim and soft warm-grey walls offsetting a Victorian piece of furniture, this focal point stated, amongst all the senescence, we had good taste. watching this one antique simply own the moment every time someone came to visit was worth the effort of its tedious arrival.

"Oh wow, where did you get that piece?" A typical question of most inviting a great story we loved to tell.

"Keith and I went to Louisville, Kentucky a couple of years ago to a wedding. In between the mass and the reception, we went antiquing—what else do you do in Louisville when you have three hours to kill?" I saw it first while Keith beamed right over toward the truck a nanosecond behind me.

"Keith look at that filthy piece of furniture they're unloading off the truck!" I screamed. "It's so cool. Stop, let's talk to the guys." An urgency in my voice decried we needed to haul a 500 lb. piece of grimy furniture back to Chicago dressed in church clothes in a Honda Civic.

"Ok, yeah it's interesting," said Keith getting excited if there is such a thing. He fell in love with it, too.

"Long story short we bought this sideboard figuring it must have originated in a church, and brought a U-Haul back to Louisville to pick it up the following weekend."

The entry arch to this room was the size of double doors, and the antique chandelier, unnoticed by many because of the show-stopping sideboard, had a street value of $2,500. according to an architect who recently visited our office. Adding a touch of history and charm, pre-war this room was the parlor. Pre-war they probably didn't have traffic like they do today in the city, therefore a selling feature of the first floor for our office was the huge picture window recently sealed and soundproofed. Above this window was a long horizontal, original stained glass window lighting up the conference room when the sun set to the west evoking a feeling of pure luxury if you enjoy antiques and the value of their spirit. The color-pop in the room, enhanced with our collection of art books, displayed in tall vertical bookshelves purposed the space as a conference room and resource library.

A major project that began two and a half years ago, stumbling around in the dark not being an authority on renovation, my knees weakened standing here oozing pride enjoying a moment of ecstasy.

"This belongs to us," saying to myself tears beginning to stream down my face hoping no one would walk in. "Wow, we did this with such a small budget." "Thanks, Mikey," saying to myself, knowing his talents and believing in me, half the credit for the results belonged to him. Hours of sweat equity and the good fortune of tasteful designers making reasonable decisions—I screamed in silence. Did the new paint fumes cause a quick dispatch of blood to my head? The rush of emotions took over my body and I let it happen. After putting out numerous fires, feeling the squeeze of unrealistic deadlines, going on tour with a new baby, this is the gift—Breathe.

The tour of inventory was officially over. I collected myself and went out the back door to my magical garden, safe haven, oasis and a myriad of other names labeling this tiny space of escape.

The meaning of a garden and working the earth can have powerful multi-tasking rewards one cannot see until they get on their hands and knees and allow themselves to get dirty. Revitalizing a backyard existing in ghetto status for several decades held meaning.

Tilling the earth making way for new growth is a symbol. Creating beds and a surface of blank dirt, eradicating weeds and amending the soil of yesteryear allowed my brain to wander, like spring cleaning my conscious being. Gardening is aerobic exercise and goes a long way in mentally sharpening your capacity to select better decisions. The blank slate of dirt, a neat canvas to visualize the crucial points of the day, week, distinguishing the relevant sound-bites and dismissing salacious insults occupying my mind. This awareness bore the juiciest fruit. I didn't possess the skill set to sit at a computer 8 hours a day staring at the screen. Feeling the madness boil up on deadlines and decisions, this place symbolized a place to throw out the trash of people's motives and pay attention to the ones with substance. Producing bright beautiful flowers pruning my senses for the next set of challenges—with a clear head.

Keith did the hardscaping—a brick walkway from scrounged bricks in a pile somewhere on the Westside of Chicago. Better known today as a highly forbidden place to enter.

"Don't ask," he liked to say when he came home with a carload of paver bricks. "Let's just say they're antiques."

"You didn't steal them?" Knowing he never had a tendency towards taking anything from someone else. Visualizing a dump site in the true ghetto of the inner-city someone led him on to and they went together for the thrill and a few bricks, enumerating several of our eclectic friends that would've enjoyed this field trip.

"Hope you took the license plates off the car before you left." Imagining the area was not particularly safe, someone might have been watching and that didn't include the police— they wouldn't go there.

August and the scorching sun of summer yielded sunflowers eight to twelve feet tall and a source of conversation for whomever walked the alley; it was impossible not to notice the beasts one to two feet in diameter.

The separation anxiety of summer turning to fall and fall to winter depressed like someone taking you to an isolation cell. Never really suffering from Seasonal Affective Disorder—only sad my sanctuary fell into remission for six solid months. The word paradise means the garden of delight. Winter in Chicago shoveling massive amounts of snow, the only outdoor recreation, meant time for indoor critical thinking.

Clearly trying feverishly to stay in front of my career, an established "good" firm in the city, the challenge was to remain that way and become notorious—a great firm supported by a team with solid systems firmly in place and qualified freelance help when we were overloaded. Absolutely abhorring sleazy business practices, integrity would become the nomenclature. My manifesto: you cannot get ahead in any venture without integrity.

14

Key Messages Resonate

Strategic by nature, I didn't expect striking balances during tedious decisions to be easy—compromising always on the table; strictly never surrendering pieces of my soul. Proving the having-it-all theory lingered out there with the judges. Giving myself a 7.5 —a score allocated to effort. The next 2.5 essentially assigned to results, striving for financial security. Searching, the points could have been assigned differently depending on perspective and time of day, however there was room for improvement.

Staying true to my original message and goals; the emerging strategy to increase the bottom line with more passive income needed to be uncovered—becoming a goal. Producing blood-knots in my brain trying to figure out how all this past work and talent came together, frazzled brain pieces occasionally allows the light bulb to go off. The exact moment of when the circuitry connects is typically out of your control. Believe. Friends and family knew I was focused on something—the intensity of my thought process appeared as shaggy charisma; searching, it appeared on my blank face with eyeballs as big as flying saucers.

Those that hold themselves in formidable esteem equally surrender themselves to being held up high for the critics to come out and take a shot at them. Like politicians who engage in this foolish behavior, it always makes me twitch. It felt like someone was stoning me while I was naked. And, it hurt. This constant criticism is part of the equation of success—I needed to get used to its ugly face. Not greedy, just enjoyed working smart.

My close friend, Mary, became a soul of refuge and kindred spirit, rarely ever criticizing, her nature was to solve problems. A salt of the earth personality, wide perfect-teeth smile and refreshing in contrast to the showmanship a design and advertising business emoted. We both drove mediocre cars, owned minimal jewelry, loved to dote on our baby girls and had deadline-oriented stressful jobs.

Residing five blocks away, a close city-friend for many years, Hannah and Amelia were born within six weeks of each other. Combining work and nurturing newborns, we consistently leaned on each other and formed a tight bond, classically soothing the working parent's nerves together—liquor on Friday night and a dose of heavy laughter—the recipe releasing pressure—laughter is an anecdote. You could hear the hissing noise for miles when the pressure valve was opened at 7pm on Friday night.

I had it all—almost. Like a detective sleuthing for a profusion of clues, the glaring message lay right in front of me. The theory of having it all was 90% solved, however something itched at my nerves—like I was teetering on an anonymous disaster. Anxiety is a force not to be reckoned with if you choose to enjoy the fruits of your labor, however listening to its nag and origination can prove to be productive. Was I leaving something on the table of my talents?

The sour fluids of yesterday's misaligned thoughts needed to be cleansed from my soul and the bath water flowing back and forth over my body assisted the transformation allowing for a fresh day to begin. "All gone," chiding to myself drying off, prepping myself for today's newness allowing a transformative moment to occur. Like hitting the refresh button for clean thinking. After all, strategic thinking was my forte and there is no dead end to the circuitry of your brain. My garden was in remission—we were heading into the holidays—time for indoor thinking without outdoor distractions.

There is no satisfactory explanation for why I never asked to be the photographer at various shoots I attended as the art director. Christmas of 1995 changed all that. "Oh my, a new lens!" squealing in delight.

Like a kid receiving their longed for toy, a possible new career path gleaned attention within seconds of opening and examining the power of this lens. Confidence in shooting well, and photos of past photography shoots in all areas of the world, I envisioned my own photo collection in layouts. Photography was evolving culturally at this time, becoming the new lifestyle use in many ads replacing illustration. A fantasy or did the light bulb go off?

"If I could take the photo, lay out the copy and assist in writing and editing the copy why would you need to source any other firm beside GKA that keeps its staff lean and the control of the details remain consistent and accurate?" asking myself. A vision of this speech encouraged the path to new ventures. Enjoying a new mantra with fearlessness has the potential to go a long way in creating a new source of income. "Legitimize why GKA could service all your visual communication needs—subtly," talking to myself.

Key messages resonated; stay on track, work smart and inhabit confidence. Listening to myself, the fine point of my true talent in a time for money model was speed. Speed keeps you competitive in this business model required to maintain your value as the vendor of choice. Speed naturally occurs when the brain has established a system. The light stayed on with a surge like a hungry tiger told to wait for their food.

"Ok, Lesley it's time. Do your magic and I'll do mine."

"We need to set up meetings with the other presidents of the banking group," Lesley noted assuring me this would enhance our firm's control of the bank's advertising and marketing needs as well as assimilating her role into my new role—the point person. The handwriting was on the wall; Lesley had plans of leaving the bank—sooner than later. She loved me like a best friend and protégé motivating her to make sure I didn't lose the entire business, instead creating new avenues for more relationships within the banking structure.

Who was I beside someone Roger and Lesley liked? We needed them, the suits in various roles, to like me and my ideas, and pay for them. Pretend I've done an intimate study on the world of banking. "A passionate artist with decent taste and a helluva salesgirl." Would that do it?

Think like the consumer; inevitably this translates to being in the know on culture, politics, the stock market, sports and a myriad of other general interest topics that might arise in a meeting. By far this generalization was my charm, a constant reader devouring information most would find boring— I could pop off a stock quote and recite the score of last night's Bulls game including Michael Jordan's stats for the night. A vast photo collection the lynchpin combining my nerd-like qualities should seal the deal. In the creative realm nerds can capture the attention of many—you would think otherwise in a business full of right brainers.

Presenting with enthusiasm and a nod to staying contemporary in the advertising environment of 1996, photography was replacing illustration as the choice for eliciting the emotions of a consumer. Highly motivated to proving this theory, anticipating the results would differentiate GKA. Specifically recalling a presentation, "Do these say vacation more than a piece of cheesy clip art of a palm tree?" Trying to be the great listener, I also became the teacher. "The world of visuals and how we relate to the printed piece is changing, and we should change with this new world." My argument that photos allow us to assimilate with the product, providing human relevance—lifestyle photography was the buzz word of the year. Illustration was subsequently turning our advertising and marketing into scrap they wrap the fish. A bold statement, we desire to appear worldly if we're going after market share. How do I say eloquently, our competitor, First National Bank of Chicago doesn't use a kangaroo? We will rise to the new standard and if I don't own the photo I can shoot the photo," remarking with a bold statement hoping no one noticed sweat oozing on my forehead like it was Africa hot and we had just run a marathon. "Change is an absolute we must adopt. Photos seek to not blur the lines between what's real and fiction. Lifestyle photos undoubtedly draw an eager audience." Exhaling these enterprising statements, longing for evaporation into thin air as a possibility.

After the delivery of a lifetime an unforgettable comment, "Linda you are certainly not dull."

"Well thank you, I've worked hard to remain a character in this cast." Laughed all the way home thinking about my compelling knockdown not truly characteristic but a boost of bold for our camp. The message of the day moving forward; be bold with confidence.

Presentations that charmed; and hoping that defying conventional use of illustration replacing these with real people in lifestyle settings as the choice of imagery, I began upping the quality of our current ads and marketing pieces with my own personal stock photos. Brave maneuvers that payed off—placing a recent, adorable non-conventional portrait of 8 month old Amelia next to the current mascot for the GreatKid's account—a well-illustrated kangaroo with money heaving out its pouch—I asked the president's of the banks, and marketing managers, "Which visual persuades grandma to open an account for grandkids?" daring to be different by asking a question thus stimulating the minds of potential new relationships. Basically flexing my creative muscle as a true competitor with the confidence of a champion. "The trend, is swiftly moving toward photography with lifestyle photos." My tenacity of purpose and relevance rewarded in a big way—the true benchmark of we like you: a generous monthly retainer and an enormous windfall of additional trust. Cash flow to count on with regularity is hard to secure—more so than the amount.

Comprehensive layouts using my own photos to give credence to why a human being spoke louder than an illustrated kangaroo, caught on quickly. Stock photos collected from sessions everyone told me "ditch the camera" (except Nancy), were used in countless ads, collateral pieces for textbooks, and consequently I became the new photographer of choice for lifestyle shots moving forward solidifying an additional service of GKA that took off like a California wildfire. Photo foibles were living in the present and receiving an income. Of the 5000 slides in my collection, at least 20 were in current use and bless their heart—they were making money.

Nerves can never sabotage prospecting new clients, it's part of the deal you signed up for when you embarked on a business. Face fear and do it with two legs to stand on—works better. We now had four legs—Keith the solid cornerstone of technology and accuracy.

At times, putting yourself out there expressing a desire to acquire new clients kindles the flame of abundance. If you keep one client happy and they go away, you are left with nothing. This is simply a model for failure, unless you have piles of stashed money to patiently wait for the next big client to show up. You may have a steel box buried in the backyard with cash, but your energy level will never match the same intensity of the first time around. Like a sprinter who develops a skill of putting themselves out there for 10 seconds, saving a miracle is headed your way, that sprinter could not turn around and do that sprint twice in a row— unless you're Jesse Owens.

Jesse Owen's achievement of setting three world records and tying another in less than an hour at the 1935 Big Ten track meet in Ann Arbor, Michigan, has been called "the greatest 45 minutes ever in sport[5] and has never been equaled.

Securing the bank for future work was an Olympic-style feat. However, the race does not end there if you want to remain relevant. Remembering to not let the river's current tear you apart, secure your life jacket to stay in front of the competition.

"Linda, the Bones Society is reviewing designers for their newsletter. Now, its probably not the pay you're used to, but it may be a foot in the door of more work," my mom casually suggesting I make an appointment for a meeting to showcase our firm.

"What does a society of bones do all day?" Asking in a humorous way clearly seeking a logical understanding of my mom's position for ten years at the American Academy of Orthopaedic Surgeons. Sincerely curious, she loved her job; focusing on her livelihood proved this moment potentially could only result in a positive outcome. Mom went back to work after raising five kids, received a degree at 51 we all applauded, and deserved a nod of approval. Naturally organized, her position at the society, reveled by many, assisted my dad in paying for five college tuitions.

Knowing her dissertation on what went down on the sixth floor of an Academy previously employing 3 brothers, considered one of the most prestigious institutions in America, could only be priceless and a true knee-slapper conscious of my mom's brilliant wit.

"We lick envelopes in the morning, and then go to lunch."

"What do you do after lunch?" chuckling with one eyebrow raised.

You get better at listening by doing it, this was an occasion my ears became huge and my mouth taped shut. "We discuss the size of the doctor's wives' wedding rings, jewelry, clothes and other issues. Linda, we are the behind-the-scenes worker bees putting together the orthopaedic surgeon's annual meetings. The details are overwhelming." The tape fell off my mouth, laughing at the visual of my mother eyeballing their jewelry.

"Each society at the Academy is responsible for a specialty society. For example, The Bones Society is the administrative arm of the other societies."

"POSNA, Pediatric Orthopaedic Society of North America,

who I work for and resides on the sixth floor with all the other specialty societies does a newsletter, keeps track of the membership and brings together all the pieces for the annual meeting. Each ortho surgeon is a specialist and they write papers for presentation at the annual meeting on the latest and greatest findings of the past year's surgeries."

"Actually, that's pretty cool, mom. So we can officially call you Dr. Mom since you must learn a lot."

"Oh, I do learn a lot," she said with her signature, sure-fire tone.

"Sheila is the head of the Bones Society and they put out an 8-12 page newsletter each quarter. She's looking to replace her current designer," siting an example of an initial possible presentation.

"Hmmm, ok."

I wasn't going to advance my career or the reputation of GKA by soliciting a new client and suggesting that the designer they currently used sucked. It would cause confusion. If we truly desired the business I had to be a pop hit with an explosive sound you hum on the way home from work. So how does one do that? I timidly sought the bottom line number from specific, interested clients and their current pay for services, developing a talent over time for eloquently finding the base of what clients paid to their current designers. In most invoices, it appeared they were offering below a figure I expected. Blowing through this number in mental math, there had to be a solution considering the current designer had employees, churned out several projects per month under this matrix and always had enough money in the budget to bring a dozen Krispy Kreme doughnuts upon arrival to visit the client. I loathed bribes—they looked fattening and felt awkward.

Was I missing something? I was turned on by seeking preferred projects. Continuing the math, viewing the numbers from a different angle, if this and what if placed in simple equations resulting in finite thinking ultimately leading to who and which client I admittedly, passionately wanted to work with. Newsletters resembled magazine design of the past—my favorite visual communication vehicle of a 16-year career to date. Passion in your work equals impact. Impact, the clue to driving my engine of desire in keeping relationships, would also differentiate our firm as the clear leader. Money became a secondary force and the ultimate gain was a juiced soul fueled by exercising a passion. Clients connected to this performance, if for nothing else it exuded a strong personal charm and a clever pathway declaring the client's final decision on who did what work. Pursuing clients to take away from others livelihood would make me look like a hog dressed in black slacks—I just wanted a piece of the pie, achieving this through enhancing the emotional experience.

Massaging type was a primary term for tenured graphic designers educated in the power of type as our ultimate communicator beyond the spoken word—we would ascend the throne and be given a BFA in Visual Communications if we promised to promote this point of view for the remainder of our lives. The anatomy of a great printed piece developed through the designer who wielded the sword and could properly persuade others as to why it must be this way is forever revered and promoted by the colleagues who also owned this sword. The computer is a form-giving tool, and the operator of this machinery, needs to be alert exercising superb form of the typographical word. In the world of policing poor visuals, you at least tried to educate others that we were communicating with someone—not to someone. We did this in the 80's and 90s. Those that were successful kept passion alive and the historical engagement of graphic design from becoming a dinosaur. This entire theory became my platform for newsletters and other forms of corporate communication at the Academy better known as AAOS.

"Yes, take this newsletter, typically eight to twelve pages, 400 finished pieces and let us know a cost, what paper you would suggest and we would most certainly like to give your firm a try. We've heard great things."

"What kind of things?" I said to myself. Pressure didn't annoy me, however, blindly meeting grandiose expectations and conquering the fear of the unruly personality you can't match wits always made me queasy. In direct contrast to negative messages, with much glee in receiving another nod of our expertise, and the prospect of expanding our business beyond the two solid clients we currently worked with on a daily basis, I knew what the upside potential promised. "Keith, there is so much work at the Academy and my mom currently promotes that we can do it—they trust her."

The what ifs of solving simple business model puzzles and creating forward momentum continued. Lesson in progress; it's easier to work with one foot forward than trying to keep your balance from the back foot. I inherited, by nature, a resilience to having information shoved down my throat. Circumventing this notion of theories of what if I did it this way and if the numbers made sense could we achieve the results necessary to sustain our business with positive momentum? Again, talking to myself and no one committed me to the looney bin, ensuring a collapse, a really good thing because people who caught a glimpse of mouth movement with no noise coming out began to ask if that's what I was doing. The push and pull of pressure whipping around from all sides—it became embarrassing.

Ah, pressure, the surefire buzzkill of all great plans. Without hitting the bottle, laughter is an amazing anecdote for the near future. Reminding myself that pressure was fleeting and if you waited it out, talked to yourself, remarkably you will become distracted from its origin. Rely on fabulous messages at this point—it will pass. "You can do this," my famous words and typical reinforcing message.

The feedback on seeking new projects universally determined the bank and the Academy wanted to write one check. Needing to be as comprehensive in the approach as possible preparing design briefs and budgets, challenges murdering my time occurred because there's a narrow line drawn between vendors and any way the proposal looked— it's guesswork. If the client liked your numbers and what you wore that day you stood a better chance. The differentiation was my confident approach at pretending. Other than this rationale, one will never know the exact science of why we are the chosen one on certain projects. The stress of little pieces out of place needed to be addressed. It's part of the pretending and then part of the making it all work. The details are the last touch you need to put on anything. Perfection is failure— reminding myself, always.

Tackling the details necessary for discovery included purchasing a high-end printer to retain the 25% mark-up, gain speed in delivery under tight deadlines and find a need for the printer beyond The Academy—and by tomorrow. "You can do this," saying to myself feeling the gnaw of pressure without being able to grasp at a concrete answer.

Needing mitigation became the upfront costs to pay the printer, freelancer and wait the 30 day lag to get paid, at times potentially 45 to 60 days. The cliché, it takes money to make money, reared its unsightly head—and we didn't have cash sitting around or buried in the backyard.

"Linda can your firm handle the printing?" Ugh. We could, but not without letting vendors sit on the sidelines waiting to be paid while we waited to be paid. Despising companies with this tacky model, my true nature wasn't about to adopt its disfigured approach to paying hard-working self-employed, freelancers at this point in my career. "Think Linda!" talking to myself—again. "Do unto others as you would have them do unto you."

Interruptions are a fact of llfe, learning to sort out what

has priority at any given second is a skill, once mastered installs trust for anyone who admires your accomplishments desiring to be part of your plan—better described as leadership qualities.

I utilized, frequently, a feeble pencil and scratch paper system to organize, prioritize and plan for durability—better spoken, "did the numbers add up correctly?" This activity occurred several times a day most days. Or, as many times as variables in the business ultimately changed—basically, every other hour. My underlining motto; do not spend feverishly without a plan. Pencil the numbers out testing if the budget was remotely correct. If they didn't work as a sketch, Excel magically couldn't prove my theories right or wrong. Receiving a D in accounting in college, leveraging Keith and his fastidious work on Excel and our certified public accountant clarified the numbers once my idea materialized verbalizing it with a rough sketch. No one relied on my addition and subtraction, just my capacity for overall creative notions and the drive to prove their authenticity. Admitting I wasn't perfect, and couldn't be responsible for being exact—the government enjoys businesses who file their taxes correctly. I've never done my own taxes and never will.

The Business Plan Reigned

The 25-page business plan! "We also need a new computer for the freelancer not to mention we need a better printer for our proofs to the client," Keith stated, knowing that growth was being inhibited by equipment well beyond our bank account and resources, but an absolute necessity for gleaming designs with a polished professional look to be exhibited. He was the expert in keeping up with technology and I was the listener and point person to put all the pieces together. Logic needed to prevail.

"If you can get me all the costs for a printer and a new workstation, we can easily plug these into the excel worksheet on the business plan, submit a proposal to the bank and acquire a line of credit necessary to float us. I'll detail the numbers for the proposal the bank's underwriters require and pray the timeframe works in our favor to get some monies. And, do the work and get paid without an interruption of losing trust in a new client. Every detail was built in to the original financial structure, now it was bearing fruit.

Keith installed a phone system wired to have calls picked up on all four floors. Amelia was upstairs with a nanny — who buzzed me, "Amelia is hungry now." Up to the third floor for breast-feeding, lunch and mommy time.

Passive income allows for relaxed freedom and a clear focus on future growth. Like peanut butter through a straw, pathways of the brain must remain liquid and not clogged by destructive messages. Expunge negative messages now! Positive messages dominate the clearest path to a future filled with abundance and your sanity.

Here is the moment you say to yourself, "Believe!" Stand directly in the middle of first-class compliments and cheap-shot insults, raise your hands to the sky and be thankful you know the difference between the two. Key messages are a glaring reminder to hold that most important visual your character can carry—integrity. Someone lurking around trying to defame your current status proving they are better than you are normal.

Keith and I loved this constant interaction and convenience of the arrangement—we adored Amelia. Together we shared the ultimate motivation in raising a child: give them self-esteem. And, we did this by being available.

The business plan was working. The Master Plan highlighting the manifesto of financial security, dismissing greed and visions of a windfall fell into place like a rehearsed concerto. Developing relationships and keeping them solid proved our ultimate financial victory. Amelia received thousands of kisses, hugs and passive income from her photos.

The formula was working. We paid ourselves a modest salary and took the profits as a bonus in order to allocate that to future growth (a faster and better printer) for producing more dramatic layouts. The operative word, drama with confidence—it sells itself every time.

"Now, I hate to be the person who told you so, but having a business plan was the smartest ingredient added to our master plan of success. No plan and we would have nothing to show the bank for a credit line. No credit line and we would have never been able to expand. No expansion and we would be beating the clock every day with the time-for-money formula, basically setting us up for burnout."

Keith was too proud to admit I was right. And I was right—officially today I wore the crown. A much-deserved summit for three solid years of following a plan, setting goals and dismissing ugly messages. Yep. I took a bow.

And it brought us in business with gleaming colors to show how much expansion, based on a plan the business displayed. Our bottom line began to double. The clients paid on time, we paid our credit line on time and maintained control over the output, including photos and copy. New relationships of trust—another moment of ecstasy. Like making new friends you like and trust—it feels good to feel good.

Amelia turned one, the ugly black-green asphalt siding turned yellow with the assistance of Michael and his bright ideas, and we turned our attention to travel and other ventures. Searching for another piece of land in Driggs, the ultimate dream on the horizon: adopting a baby. In 1997 we bought a glorious 9-acre piece of property in Driggs, directly under the Teton range and began our pursuit of adopting a baby in Russia. By the time we put a comprehensive dossier together required to meet the demands of adopting, presented our business including the life we meticulously put together we went to the front of the line to adopt from a country threatening to close its adoptions.

Author Biography

Linda, a Visual Communication expert ran a successful design and advertising firm in the city of Chicago for 15 years. Combining her branding and marketing skills with her award-winning photos, copywriting and design talents, her projects ranged from retail to banking to textbook publishing.

Earning her BFA from the University of Kansas, she is a Chicago native. Linda began her career in corporate communications for a design firm in the beatnik section of the city in the early 80's known today as *the* trendy River North gallery district. Best-described as a graphic designer from the beginning, she enjoyed a successful run delivering several high-profile multi-level collateral programs for Beatrice Foods including their corporate magazine. Furthering her career she moved in to consumer magazines art directing for *Outside Magazine, Chicago Magazine* and the *Chicago Tribune.*

Linda excels in her ability to connect with client's in their process of presenting information keeping the message clear. Most tenured graphic designers also fell under the titles of art director/designer/creative director/photographer/copywriter—they are all essential in the end product. Linda understands that selling the product includes creating the product and this paradigm demands wearing many hats simultaneously. Currently focusing her talents on writing, believing the copy drives the idea and a message—the message in Having It All or Not?: plans work, messages to ourselves are effective ways to the desired results. No plan, plan to fail.

Seeking a better life and more freedom, her wit and wisdom are motivators for those desiring a higher level of existence. She writes as if you're joining her along the adventures reminding readers that they are not so different than she is—guilty pleasures and all. You sense her passion to share something in her writing making her relatable. A self-described information geek with a photographic memory including a mini-career in gardening she swears assisted in soothing the nerves from the frenzied pace of living and working in a big city.

Bibliography

(works consulted)

1   *The Speed of Trust,* Stephen M. R. Covey, ©2006, ISBN 13-978-0-7432-9730-I
2   *The Tipping Point,* Malcom Gladwell, ©2002, ISBN 0-31696-2 (HC)
3   (works verbatim from Wikipedia qualifying the story) *Beatrice Foods, Mergers and Acquisitions, Wikipedia,* 1985
4   (works verbatim from Wikipedia qualifying the story) *Great Chicago Flood of 1992, Wikipedia,* 1992
5   (works verbatim from Wikipedia qualifying the story) *Jesse Owens Olympic Feat 1942, Wikipedia,* 1942

Printed in the United States
By Bookmasters